Making Jesus Attractive

Making Jesus Attractive
The Ministry and Message of Young Life

Gretchen Schoon Tanis

Foreword by
Pete Ward

☙PICKWICK *Publications* • Eugene, Oregon

MAKING JESUS ATTRACTIVE
The Ministry and Message of Young Life

Copyright © 2016 Gretchen Schoon Tanis. All rights reserved. Except for brief quotations in critical publications or reviews, no part of this book may be reproduced in any manner without prior written permission from the publisher. Write: Permissions. Wipf and Stock Publishers, 199 W. 8th Ave., Suite 3, Eugene, OR 97401.

Pickwick Publications
An Imprint of Wipf and Stock Publishers
199 W. 8th Ave., Suite 3
Eugene, OR 97401

www.wipfandstock.com

PAPERBACK ISBN: 978-1-62564-166-3
HARDCOVER ISBN: 978-1-4982-8782-1

Cataloguing-in-Publication Data

Schoon Tanis, Gretchen.

Making Jesus attractive : the ministry and message of Young Life / Gretchen Schoon Tanis ; foreword by Pete Ward.

xii + 168 p. ; 23 cm. Includes bibliographical references.

ISBN 978-1-62564-166-3 (PAPERBACK) | ISBN 978-1-4982-8782-1 (HARDCOVER)

1. Young Life Campaign. 2. Church work with youth. I. Ward, Pete, 1959–. II. Title.

BV4447 .S24 2016

Manufactured in the U.S.A.   02/01/2016

This book is dedicated to my community of saints JMS and MDY. This book is also dedicated to my children who were gifts from God in the midst of this project, Jon and M. E. And I dedicate this book to my husband, Phil, who would not appreciate an overabundance of hype so I simply say thank you and I love you.

Contents

Foreword by Pete Ward | ix
Acknowledgments | xi

1 History | 1
2 Formal Doctrine | 51
3 Incarnational Theology: Christology, Soteriology, Campaigners | 72
4 Cultural Expression | 100
5 Conclusions and Recommendations | 147

Bibliography | 161

Foreword

THIS IS QUITE SIMPLY a groundbreaking book. It is the first in-depth study of the ministry and message of one of the most important parachurch youth ministry organizations in the United States. *Making Jesus Attractive* gives us a cultural take on the theology of Young Life—cultural in that it focuses on the distinctive forms of expression and communication that have been developed by Young Life as the means to share the faith with young people.

Jim Rayburn, the founder of Young Life, famously said, "It's a sin to bore a kid with the gospel."[1] This much-quoted youth ministry maxim contains in a nutshell the genius of Young Life. The challenge that Rayburn set down was to find a way to make a connection between the gospel and young people without being dull. Gretchen Schoon Tanis shows how Young Life is built around the belief that the message of Jesus Christ should be shared in ways that resonate with where young people are at. So it isn't just that the youth minister has to "earn the right to be heard" through building long term relationships with young people. The gospel message and indeed what it means to be a disciple of Christ has to be presented as the opposite of what it is to be boring. This commitment to not be boring has given a cultural spin to the way that the Christian faith is communicated by Young Life.

In *Making Jesus Attractive* Gretchen Schoon Tanis takes us on the Young Life roller coaster. She shows how Rayburn's gospel vision was expressed in cultural forms—how Young Life clubs developed a fun and engaging way to share Christ and how the Young Life camps tried to ensure that this was the best week in every young person's life. She sets out how Young Life promoted its work through pictures and stories that went all

---

1. Meredith, *It's a Sin to Bore a Kid.*

out to make Jesus attractive to young people. She tells us how the gospel message was honed and developed by successive Young Life leaders into an enduring way of sharing Christ with young people through a set pattern of stories and illustrations. In short, she develops an affectionate and an insider's account of Young Life's cultural theology.

Gretchen is a Young Life insider. She came to faith through attending a Young Life club and going to camp, and then as a young believer she attended Campaigners. As a young adult she was a Young Life leader. She is Young Life family. It is as family then that she affectionately and appreciatively describes the theological communication of Young Life. But it is also as family that she shares her concerns about the way that particular forms of cultural expression have given a distinctive theological spin to the message and ministry of Young Life. Her critical examination of Young Life may be read by some as controversial, but I know that it has been written out of a commitment to the gospel of Jesus Christ and a love for young people and those in the organization who give their lives in ministry.

This is an important and timely book. Theologically, this is an important book because it is an in-depth examination of how communicative practices generate distinctive theological perspectives. It is important for Young Life because it challenges the organization to reflect on how it shares the faith. It is timely because the 75th anniversary of the organization should be a time to reflect on the past and reset the compass for the future. For the wider Church it is important because it shines a light on youth ministry as a place where distinctive forms of gospel expression have been forged, and it asks questions about how accountable, in terms of theology, parachurch agencies should be in the future.

Pete Ward

Professor of Practical Theology, MF Norwegian School of Theology
Professorial Fellow, Durham University

Acknowledgments

FIRST I WOULD LIKE to thank my advisor Pete Ward for his patience and long-suffering. He always had the right thing to say, and this project would not be what it is without his wisdom. Thank you, Pete, for being willing to take me on as your student and for covering for me for so many years!

I would like to thank the Young Life organization whose hospitality and care enabled me to do the research I needed to for this study. At all times they welcomed me and encouraged me in my work, offering all they could that would benefit this project. I am indebted to Terry Swenson and Krina Roxman from Young Life headquarters for their help in locating items in the archives and their willingness to answer many questions! Arnie and Mary Lou Jacobs warmly received me upon each visit to Colorado Springs. Thank you for your warm reception and hospitality. I would also like to thank those from Holland (Michigan) Area Young Life who allowed me to interview them, observe ministries, and spend hours in conversation about the state of the ministry in our community as they seek to reach young people with the Good News of Jesus Christ. May God continue to bless your ministry.

My home away from home over these many years was the library at Hope College. It cannot be overstated that I come from a community that encourages higher learning. Thank you to all of the staff who helped in my research and especially Carla Kaminski who was my lifeline and ever-present encourager at the library. Thank you for making the library a conducive environment in which to work.

There are many friends for whom this journey would have been impossible without their encouragement, support, listening ear, prayer, and pastoral care. I wish to thank my brothers in Christ, Jack Gabig and Nick

Acknowledgments

Shepherd, who went before me to pave the way. Without you I would have been lost. I also wish to thank my SGs: Kathy Schoon Tanis, Kristen Johnson, and Deb VanDuinen. You are indeed smart, classy women who carry life as mothers, academics and Christ-followers with grace and laughter. Thank you for sharing your lives with me!

This project is dedicated to both of my families. First to the Schoon family and especially my dad Jon Mark Schoon whose legacy made this project possible. He exhibited a dedication for doing things well and I hope this project would make him proud. And to the Tanis family for their sense of uprightness and adventure. Thank you for your love and sacrifice and support.

1
History

It is a black-and-white photo from the 1950s and it is a picture of Jim Rayburn, the founder of Young Life. He is dressed casually in khaki pants and a comfortable shirt as he leans up against the wall of the room. As he stands, hundreds of high school students are packed into the room sitting on the floor around his feet.

As I read the article that accompanies this photograph it says that Young Life is so popular in this town that the only space that is large enough to hold club is the local mortuary. More than three hundred young people gather to listen to Jim Rayburn speak to them about Jesus Christ.[1] And this is not the only photograph of this kind. As I discover more and more stories of the early years of Young Life the same story resonates: Jim Rayburn is such a dynamic speaker that he often packs out rooms with young people who clamor to hear him tell stories about this person Jesus Christ. Whether it is the mortuary from this photograph, hotel ballrooms, or living rooms of large houses, Jim Rayburn has a way of attracting teenagers to hear the Good News of the gospel.

In this chapter I lay out the cultural trends that led to the formation of the Young Life organization as well as the influences of founder Jim Rayburn and the projection of the ministry since its formation in 1941. However, Young Life was not a solitary organization when formed in the 1940s; it joined a number of other evangelical youth ministries that were being established at that time. This chapter describes in detail the cultural trends that led to the parallel formation of evangelical youth ministries in the United States in the 1940s that were influential in forming the Christian identity of young people. Three main cultural trends shaped the structure of these groups: the evolving nuances of the evangelical church, the golden era of teenagers of the 1940s, and post-WWII patriotic momentum with a fervor of Christian revival. These three trends helped shape the formation of not only Young Life but also the Miracle Book Club, Youth for Christ, and InterVarsity Christian Fellowship.[2] Though Young Life was formed in a parallel manner to other evangelical youth organizations, I will show that Young Life had specific influences that shaped their ministry and led to the current trajectory today. I will specifically address the influences of founder Jim Rayburn and the mark that he placed on the ministry of Young Life. But Young Life has moved beyond the foundational elements of Jim Rayburn, and I will address current trends in the ministry that has shaped the Young Life organization.

---

1. *Young Life* magazine, November 1952, 22.

2. In the midst of the Second World War, three important evangelical, non-denominational, national youth-oriented organizations were established in the United States: Youth for Christ, InterVarsity Christian Fellowship, and Young Life. They are important because "between them, these three organizations drew thousands of young people to rallies, small-group meetings, and Bible studies throughout the forties and fifties" (Pahl, *Youth Ministry in Modern America*, 58).

History

I also show the influencing factors of the evangelical church of the 1900s that led to independent non-denominational organizations such as the youth organizations discussed. Here I illustrate the importance of biblical foundation that was emphasized by the evangelical church using InterVarsity Christian Fellowship. I explain that the emphasis of InterVarsity ministry represents the biblical foundation that formed the character of evangelical youth ministry. In the second section I discuss the golden era of teenagers illustrating the emergence of the adolescent, the role of the public high school, and the teenage consumer culture. Here the Miracle Book Club represents the emerging evangelical ministry that focused on the campus of the public school as it grew in importance in the 1930s and 40s. Because more and more young people were being educated in the public school, evangelical ministries began to focus their emphasis on or near the school campus. In the third section, post-WWII revivals, I discuss the fervor Christian leaders had for witnessing for Christ in the decades during and just after the Second World War. Here I argue that the ministry of Youth for Christ represents the importance placed on rallies and youth culture that was utilized in order to influence young people for Christ. Through their use of entertaining rallies and fast-paced proclamations of the gospel, Youth for Christ is an example of evangelical youth ministry and its emphasis on entertaining ministry and mass appeals in presenting Christ to young people.

I focus my attention on the foundation and ministry of Young Life, first discussing the founder of the ministry Jim Rayburn. Because of specific factors that shaped his life, I argue Jim Rayburn had a specific and lasting influence on the ministry. I also outline the specifics of the Young Life organization including historical details and components of the ministry. Through this movement I illustrate that, despite Young Life organizing during a similar season as other evangelical youth ministries, the ministry of Young Life leaves a distinct mark on and was innovative of youth ministry in the United States. The Young Life organization was adding its distinct mark to the youth parachurch movement within the United States in the early 1940s, including this new attitude towards relationships as argued by Root. However, the emergence of Young Life as a youth movement has as much to do with the influence of its founder as it does with the state of the evangelical church at the time. The history of the organization begins with the fundamental upbringing of founder Jim Rayburn and his formation growing up within an evangelical family.

As Pahl states, there have been changing streams in the Christian tradition of the United States, as well as distinct Christian life-paths that have been communicated to young people in the United States in the twentieth century.[3] Within this chapter I will show the various streams that have led to the Christian paths of witness that have influenced the evangelical Christian organizations that work with young people in the United States as they formed in the early twentieth century. As I do this, I set out the parallel formation of organizations but also the distinct trends that shaped the Young Life Campaign.

Parallel Formation

Marsden argues that there is an overall evangelical pattern made up of diverse pieces and uses the term "evangelical mosaic" to describe the movement. He argues that many American evangelicals participate in this larger historical pattern, whether they acknowledge it or not, because they share a common heritage within the evangelical movement. Marsden argues for evangelicalism to be considered a movement rather than a category because of common heritages, tendencies, and identity that often tie evangelical bodies together in an organic manner. Though these evangelical subgroups might not acknowledge other groups or their connections to the larger evangelical movement, this common heritage connects them even in the midst of their independence.[4] The ecclesiological and cultural characteristics discussed in this chapter will give foundation for the specific evangelical guidelines that were necessary as parachurch organizations forged their ministries in the early 1940s. Marsden goes on to state that evangelicals in the United States have generally moved in similar directions because they have been shaped by the democratic society that favors individuality and optimistic views of human nature. He also notes that evangelicals, shaped by American norms, often put into practice the popular cultural trends that influence their message.[5]

As I consider the ecclesiological characteristics that have forged the identity of evangelical youth ministries in the United States, I first look at the history of the evangelical church that led to the formation of independent youth organizations in the 1940s. Within evangelical youth ministries,

   3. Pahl, *Youth Ministry in Modern America*, 4.
   4. Marsden, *Evangelicalism and Modern America*.
   5. Ibid.

there is a common heritage shared from the foundation of the church. Here I argue that because of the changes in the make up of the evangelical church, independent youth organizations were organized as a result of the shift in denominational make up.

Evangelical History of the Church

The first stream of influence that led to the formation of nondenominational Christian youth organizations was the schism that took place between the fundamentalist and modernist churches of the 1920s. During that decade, evangelicalism, or the evangelical movement, in the United States is often attributed to the debate and theological struggle surrounding the Scopes monkey trial.[6] The Scopes monkey trial has come to be identified as the narrow-mindedness of conservative Christianity in the United States.[7] Hart breaks down the Protestant evangelical experience in the United States into three historical periods: the first period runs roughly from 1900 to the 1920s when practices of Protestants who today would be called evangelicals were indistinguishable from mainline Protestants of the time. During the 1920s the second period of evangelical Protestant experience began to take shape. Hart recognizes this as the decade when the fundamentalist-modernist controversy erupted around the Scopes monkey trial. The third period comes after the 1920s as a result of this controversy and opened the landscape to parachurch organizations formed outside of denominational influence. This has proven to be the crucial expression of evangelical Christianity as we recognize it in the United States today. Hart states that Protestants at that time

> . . . insisted, contrary to liberal thought, that Christianity demanded renunciation of the world. The task of all believers was to save sinners from worldliness and demonstrate biblical holiness.

---

6. In 1925 the state of Tennessee brought to trial John T. Scopes—a local high school science teacher who taught evolution in the classroom. The state of Tennessee had previously passed a law prohibiting any teaching that denied the story of Divine Creation as found in the Bible. Scopes was found guilty, but the "liberal" media had passed their own judgment on the proceedings—speaking out against the "backwardness" of the beliefs and proceedings of the trial (Hart, *That Old-Time Religion in Modern America*).

7. As noted by Marsden, the English response to the Scopes Monkey Trial was seen as inconceivable. He quotes, "Perhaps no recent event in America stands more in need of explanation, wrote a British observer in 1925" (Marsden, "Fundamentalism," 305).

... From the fundamentalists'[8] perspective, the liberal effort ... represented a break with true evangelical tradition of reforming society through changed lives.[9]

This controversy between fundamental and liberal churches would be momentous in forming the character of the third period of evangelicalism in the United States. Because evangelical Christians broke from previous Protestant structures, fundamental and evangelical successors did not carry forward the history of nineteenth-century American Christianity. Hart argues that twentieth-century evangelicals, although similar in thought and understanding to the nineteenth-century church, had to act very differently, creating structures from scratch amidst the circumstances facing them in twentieth-century America.[10] Martin Marty agrees, noting that defeats in these denominational conflicts of the 1920s forced fundamentalists (as we now refer to as evangelicals) to strengthen their institutional structures outside of traditional denominational lines.[11] Christian Smith notes that the total effect of the fundamentalist-modernist controversy was powerful and conspicuous. By the end of the 1930s, much of conservative Protestantism—under the banner of fundamentalism—had evolved into a somewhat reclusive and defensive version of its nineteenth-century self. Organizationally, fundamentalism was expanding and strengthening. But in spirit and culture, much of fundamentalism seemed to have become "withdrawn, defensive, judgmental, factionalized, brooding, self-righteous, anti-intellectual, paranoid, and pessimistic. At least that is how things looked to some of the younger, more moderate fundamentalist leaders at the time. The conditions were ripe for a countermovement from within."[12] And Marsden states that because of the furious battles that took place in the 1920s to control denominations and the wider culture, fundamentalists were forced to become more separatist, forming independent churches and agencies.[13]

This impulse to create new evangelical structures, then, became influential for the parachurch organizations that emerged in the 1940s and

---

8. Marsden states that the term fundamentalism is a twentieth-century movement that was closely tied to Protestant revivalism but was militantly opposed to modernist theology and the cultural changes that came with the modernist bent (ibid., 303).

9. Hart, *That Old-Time Religion*, 19.

10. Ibid., 20.

11. Marty, *Growing Up Postmodern*.

12. Smith, *American Evangelicalism*, 9.

13. Marsden, "Fundamentalism," 304.

History

1950s in the United States. The Young Life organization and other youth ministries were a part of these new structures. Carpenter makes the connection between the evangelical movement in the United States with the parachurch pattern of associational life that was adopted by that movement. Evangelicals, instead of forcing followers to choose between fundamentalism and denominational life, shifted their alliance to independent ministries while maintaining membership in older denominations. This began a pattern of forming special-purpose parachurch groups to accomplish religious purposes.[14]

One characteristic of the emerging shift of fundamentalist/evangelical churches was the reliance on Scripture, not the church, for authority. Marsden states, "Lacking a strong institutional church and denying the relevance of much of Christian tradition, American Protestants were united behind the principle of *Scriptura sola*. Indeed, the Bible played a major role in America's self-understanding. . . . The true church should set aside all intervening tradition, and return to the purity of New Testament practice. The Bible alone should be one's guide."[15] This Biblicism combined with an understanding of faith as a vehicle for saving souls, encouraged revivalism[16] and vice versa, strengthened religious individualism. "The individual stood alone before God; his choices were decisive. The church, while important as a supportive community, was made up of free individuals. The Bible,[17] moreover, was a great equalizer. With Bible in hand, the common man or woman could challenge the highest temporal authority."[18] Not only did this Biblicism encourage charismatic leaders to found their organizations on the authority of the Bible alone, but it would also impact the nature and

---

14. Carpenter, *Revive Us Again*.

15. Marsden, *Fundamentalism and American Culture*, 224.

16. Revivals became a hallmark of these organizations' early work. "Billy Graham's crusades and other agents of revivalism such as Youth for Christ were not merely throwbacks to the Billy Sunday era [of the 1920s]. They were the postwar descendants of a continuing revival tradition preserved and transformed by the fundamentalist movement. . . . [R]evivalism had not died during the depression. Rather, the fundamentalist movement nurtured that tradition, introduced innovations and produced a new generation of revivalists" (Marty, *Accounting for Fundamentalism*, 67).

17. Young Life founder Jim Rayburn echoes this sentiment in a statement made to church leaders in 1962. "Renewal—revival—I don't care which term you use—I am not afraid of nomenclature if it does not obscure or tone down the biblical impact of what we are talking about. Renewal is all right with me, but I still prefer just plain revival" (Rayburn, Chicago Fellowship transcript).

18. Marsden, *Fundamentalism and American Culture*, 224.

shape of organizations such as Youth for Christ and InterVarsity Christian Fellowship in terms of their ministry goals.

One example of this biblically based, individualistic outreach in youth ministries can be seen in the InterVarsity Christian Fellowship.[19] The first important tenet of InterVarsity was the establishment of their movement as one of "evangelizing fellowship." They believed in the priesthood of all believers, and encouraged Christian students on university campuses to carry the responsibility of the gospel—InterVarsity would be a student movement.[20] Hunt argues that this philosophy of student work was a distinctive characteristic for InterVarsity. Arguing that the conservative Christian church was in isolation mode in the late 1930s because of the liberal and modern controversies, Hunt believes InterVarsity was setting the trend for encouraging Christian young people to take responsibility not only for their faith but in sharing that faith with others.[21] In practice, InterVarsity emphasized personal quiet time, corporate Bible study, and outreach and evangelism of peers. Hunt believes that "The InterVarsity movement came as a new kind of Christianity, a deeper, a more life-encompassing relationship with God through Christ than we had ever known before."[22]

> The unique mark of InterVarsity on the parachurch landscape of the 1940s and 1950s would be their emphasis on student-led evangelical outreach. Though other parachurch organizations like Youth for Christ were utilizing the emerging youth culture of that time, InterVarsity had less of a response to this phenomenon than others. InterVarsity considered university students to be young

---

19. InterVarsity Christian Fellowship in the United States was an import from the evangelical student societies of Cambridge and London in the late nineteenth century. InterVarsity of Britain was an alternative to the Student Christian Movement of the time, and would continue the function of conservative evangelical alternative as it moved into Canada and the United States. The British student leaders, wanting to organize chapters in Canadian universities in the early twentieth century, commissioned Howard Guinness, a medical student, to pioneer the work in 1928. By 1934 C. Stacey Woods, an Australian graduate student from Wheaton College, took over the work of InterVarsity and led to the expansion into the United States. One of the first chapters to be established by Woods in the United States was on the campus of the University of Michigan, and was helped by businessman Herbert J. Taylor who helped with financial support as well as organizational leadership. "During the following decade this organization grew rapidly, to nearly 200 campus chapters in 1945 and over 550 by 1950" (Carpenter, *Revive Us Again*, 183).

20. Hunt, *For Christ and the University*, 78.

21. Ibid.

22. Ibid., 85.

adults and thus, as considered by InterVarsity, able to bear responsibility for the movement. During the post-war years that marked the emergence of so many parachurch organizations focusing on youth, there was amazing response within InterVarsity to the call of mission work and evangelism that had a revitalizing effect on the religious life of the country.[23]

However, the existence of these new special-purpose parachurch organizations began to compete for religious identity within Protestantism. Although concentrating on specialized activities or people groups, parachurch organizations were supposed to work in conjunction with the church. But as the twentieth century progressed, the evangelical subculture of parachurch ministries began to compete for attention.[24] Christian Smith provides a glimpse of the numerous agencies that emerged as special purpose ministries in the midst of this growing subculture:

> The growing host of evangelical missions and evangelistic ministries came to include Youth for Christ, Campus Crusade for Christ, Young Life, InterVarsity Christian Fellowship, The Navigators, Teen Challenge, Fellowship of Christian Athletes, World Vision International, the Lausanne Committee for World Evangelization, the Overseas Missionary Fellowship, the Evangelical Foreign Missions Association, and the World Evangelical Fellowship, again just to name a few.... In a relatively short time, then, the evangelical movement had established an institutional infrastructure of impressive magnitude and strength.[25] [Footnote by Marsden 1984, "Institutionally, this trans-denominational evangelicalism is built around networks of parachurch agencies."]

The schism that took place between the fundamentalist and modernist churches in the United States after the Scopes Monkey Trial of 1925 led to the formation of independent evangelical bodies because the fundamentalists were no longer associating with denominational churches or their agencies. Because of this momentum, the ground was cleared for independent organizations such as Young Life, Youth for Christ, InterVarsity, and others to form in the 1930s and 1940s. Evangelical, non-denominational, special purpose organizations were one trend that emerged as a formative power for Young Life and others, but a cultural trend that was emerging around

---

23. Ibid.
24. Hart, *That Old-Time Religion in Modern America*.
25. Smith, *American Evangelicalism*, 13.

Golden Era of the Teenager

Adolescence

Having articulated the foundation for independent evangelical organizations after the fundamentalist/modernist schism, it is important to note that organizations such as Young Life or Youth for Christ would not be necessary if there not a group of people they felt needed to be "reached for Christ." The articulation of the term and understanding of adolescence provided the foundation for outreach. While the concepts of "adolescence" and "teenager" as we know them today did not develop fully until the first half of the twentieth century, we can see their origins throughout the nineteenth century—in both Christian and secular arenas. Trends began which contributed to the climate necessary for the development of this new concept of adolescent—no longer a child, yet not quite an adult.

> Adolescence is, by definition, a dependent state, experienced in one's own household and in institutions intended for people in their teens. As it developed in nineteenth-century America, however, adolescence did require a measure of at least psychological liberation by the parents. They had to understand that their children would be, in some important ways, different from themselves.[26]

Joseph Kett, his work on documenting the history of adolescence, notes that a change in the tradition of influencing young people for God began in the early to mid-1800s. Due to pressure to exhibit a religious change in lifestyle, revivals began focusing on teenaged conversion. "Most of the converts in revivals during the early 19th century were in their teens or early 20s."[27] Revivals attracted and most often affected teens in large numbers, so young people themselves often instigated them. In New England in the early 1800s, fifteen of twenty-four revivals were initiated by young people.[28]

---

26. Hine, *Rise and Fall of the American Teenager*, 96.
27. Kett, *Rites of Passage*, 64.
28. Ibid., 64.

In upstate New York so many revivals moved through the area like wildfires that it was referred to as the Burnt Over District.[29]

"By the 1830s evangelical Sunday schools were deemphasizing mere memorization of biblical verses in favor of direct efforts to promote conversions, while college revivals, rare in the 18th century, were becoming virtually annual rituals, as predictable as spring's first warbler."[30] The emphasis was on converting young people, from children to college-aged adult, and it was concluded this could be done en masse. The revivals and evangelical movement set in motion a religious practice that became foundational both theologically and institutionally (and would be taken up again by Youth for Christ, Young Life, and others in the next century).

This is not to say that parents were uninvolved in their children's lives. A significant shift in the bourgeoisie class of America to having fewer children was a key component in the evolution of the teenager that we know today. Parental energy shifted from young people as a source of income to a focus of development. Because families were able to survive without the income of young people, investment in education became the emphasis. The teen years, therefore, became an age for preparation for life rather than a lifetime of employment.[31] The shifting emphasis toward preparing children for adulthood rather than employment was also a focus of the Christian revivalist movement in the late nineteenth and early twentieth century, as the revivalists looked to encourage maturation in Christ as part of the development of adolescence.

This generation was the first to experience the theories (and practices) pioneered by G. Stanley Hall and others. "Hall, psychologist and college president, didn't invent the American teenager. But his vision of adolescence as a beautiful and perilous time still exerts a powerful influence over the way we see the young."[32] Recognizing the fervor with which young people were converted by evangelistic crusades, Hall was led to formulate ideas on the uniqueness of youth that made them open to such religious persuasion. He postulated that conversion in young people was spontaneous—arising from biological changes and social imperatives. He concluded that religious conversion was a product of sexual maturation, even calculating the age of conversion to be 16. Hall argued for an extension of the age

---

29. Hine, *Rise and Fall of the American Teenager*, 96.
30. Kett, *Rites of Passage*, 66.
31. Hine, *The Rise and Fall of the American Teenager*.
32. Ibid., 158.

of adolescence so that possibilities of young people could be realized. Hall viewed adolescence as a time of hyperactivity, social sensibility, and self-absorption. Young people were moving away from the harmony of childhood but were not yet ready for adulthood. Hall postulated that a removal of adult-like responsibilities and behavior would allow young people the normal outgrowth of biological maturation.[33] This was a striking change from the last century. In just a couple of generations, teen-aged individuals had gone from being an important part of a family's economic survival to becoming wholly dependent on adult-created institutions—at least in middle-class homes. Formerly burdened by adult responsibilities, these youth were now given freedom, albeit restricted and directed, to grow up more slowly and deliberately. But to speak of adolescence as something discovered would be a misnomer, as adolescence was essentially a term imposed on youth as a conception of behavior rather than an assessment of how they actually behaved. Kett describes a set of norms that was linked to adolescence–the inculcation of "school spirit," implanting "loyalty," and "hero worship"[34] in team sports amongst boys.[35]

Because of the influence of Hall and the understanding that young people needed to have a separate time of growth, more and more institutions were created during the late nineteenth and early twentieth centuries to work specifically with young people. With the energy and commitment of adult sponsors, a number of institutions came to prominence during this time. The YMCA, Christian Endeavor, Boy Scouts, and other Christian missions all capitalized on the articulation of Hall's impresionable adolescent.

The Public High School

Hall's theories that set in motion the popular belief that all young people should be in school while also giving guidance for how those schools should be managed. This fundamental change coincided with technological advances that made jobs scarcer, thus sending young people to school in

---

33. Kett, *Rites of Passage*.

34. Meredith states, "Part of the technique was to find quality people who could be paraded as hero models before the high school assemblies. Gil Dodds was one. At that time he held the world's indoor record in running the mile. And he was a Christian. He traveled with Jim [Rayburn] through Texas, Colorado and on to the west coast" (Meredith, *It's a Sin to Bore a Kid*, 36).

35. Kett, *Rites of Passage*.

higher numbers. Educational reform laws—limiting the number of hours young people could work and making education for older children compulsory—also came into effect during this time.

Many of these impulses had been bubbling around in the middle class during the final two decades of the 1800s. These attitudes and concepts "now pushed beyond the perimeters of that class in the shape of efforts to universalize and to democratize the concept of adolescence. A biological process of maturation became the basis of the social definition of an entire age group."[36] Public high schools became an institution that were dedicated to not only educational instruction but catalyzing the process of maturation as well. High schools began to offer competitive sports, activities and dances and other special events. Though there had been a number of such organizations created by young people in conjunction with the local school, organizations run by adults began to supplant these during this time. Hine states that the "overall effect was to make people in their teens into a distinctive group that was less often relied upon—even by itself—to take responsibility and make its own decisions."[37] The high school evolved into a self-contained world creating this distinct group—the teenager.

The first two decades of the twentieth century saw Hall's theories become institutionalized, culminating in the high school. "By the 1930s, active high school students did little more than eat and sleep at home. . . . [and] popularity was already the measure of true high school success."[38] But most teenagers still worked for a living—the middle class had not yet blossomed into its post-World War II prime. These teenage workers "were not considered teenagers yet, or even adolescents for that matter—the terms only applied to high school students at the time. They were teenage children who could expect to be seen but not heard within their family circle and ignored, for the most part, outside of it."[39] The expansion and influence of the high school came in the form of the Great Depression—one avenue that could alleviate unemployment amongst young people. "In the 1930s attendance at high school became a kind of cure for inflated unemployment rates among teenagers."[40] And then came the Second World War, radically transforming especially the middle and bottom half of American society. In

---

36. Ibid., 215.
37. Hine, *Rise and Fall of the American Teenager*, 163.
38. Palladino, *Teenagers*, 8–9.
39. Ibid., 5.
40. Kett, *Rites of Passage*, 264.

the 1940s and following World War II, the high school was becoming the influential factor in the life of adolescents, with 80 percent of teenagers enrolled. With jobs going to returning war veterans, young people were turning to public education for training. "Education, for the first time widely available to children of the working and lower classes, was heralded as the ticket to 'abundant life.'"[41]

With more young people attending high school, the Miracle Book Club was founded in 1933 and was the parachurch organization that preceded the formation of Youth for Christ, InterVarsity, and Young Life to become the first organization to work specifically with high school students and the emerging environment of the high school campus. The Miracle Book Club characterizes the shift of independent evangelical youth ministries to focus attention on the public school and its students—establishing Christian ministry on or near the school campus. The founder of the Miracle Book Club, Evelyn McClusky, is considered to be a pioneer of the parachurch movement in the United States.[42] McClusky was invited to start a Bible club for high school students in Oregon after religious instruction was banned from public schools in the US.[43] McClusky desired to see young people reached who were not involved in church, and her unique style of teaching the Bible set the Miracle Book Club apart from any other school activity. The Miracle Book Club became a national movement as its reputation spread through the *Sunday School Times*—a magazine devoted to Christian work done with young people (and in itself an example of how Christians were focused on work with youth). The Miracle Book Club peaked with over 1,000 clubs nationally and influenced future Christian leaders[44]

---

41. Shultze, *Dancing in the Dark*, 80.

42. Senter, *The Coming Revolution in Youth Ministry*.

43. "The dual movements of students out of the home and into the high school while religious instruction was being removed from the public school left a vacuum of religious and moral instruction. The trend which gradually increased during the period set the stage for a response on the part of Christian adults" (Senter, *The Coming Revolution in Youth Ministry*, 109).

44. The Miracle Book Club can claim an impressive array of twentieth-century Christian leaders as part of its work in the early days. Edith and Francis Schaeffer (L'Abri founders) were MBC directors for Pennsylvania in 1939, Jim Rayburn of Young Life was state director for Texas in 1940, Al Metsker and Jack Hamilton (who went on to form Youth for Christ club program) were leaders in the Kansas City chapter in 1941 (Senter, *The Coming Revolution in Youth Ministry*).

such as Jim Rayburn, who was a Miracle Book Club state director[45] for Texas in 1940.[46]

Consumer Culture

With more and more young people segregated into their high school environment, another distinct phenomenon emerged. Young people began to inhabit a consumer culture based on their experiences and persuasions. Shelley states, "[The teenager] has roles and values and ways of behaving all its own. It emphasizes sexual attractiveness, immediate pleasure, and comradeship in a way that is belligerently non-adult. After World War II, catering to this teenage market emerged as the nation's commercial passion."[47] Economic changes—creating a prosperous middle class and lightening the financial burdens of lower class families—combined with educational reform, legal changes, and psychological theories and insights to create what has been termed the "classic period of the American teenager," lasting from just before World War II to the beginning of the conflict in Vietnam.[48] Grace Palladino claims the generation of bobby soxers, those listening to jazz and swing music in the late 1930s and early 1940s, as the beginning of this adolescent culture. For the first time young people had the financial resources (and the products available on which to spend those resources) that were separate from parental control.

Just as young people were emerging as a powerful force in the market economy, World War II began and drastically shifted responsibilities and roles of teenagers in America. Young men were off to fight in the war and young women took on greater responsibility in the home as their mothers

---

45. Rayburn's role as state director for the Miracle Book Club was short-lived. He joined MBC in the spring of 1939 and by 1941 had split from the organization. The methods of the MBC were at odds with how Rayburn liked to run clubs for students. One of Rayburn's early associates, Ted Benson, stated that Miracle Book Clubs were effeminate and ineffective for reaching non-Christian high school students because it was all "lilies and lace" (Sublett, *The Diaries of Jim Rayburn*, 74). The split with the Miracle Book Club was not a cordial one. Rayburn received a scathing letter from the president of the organization and as things were winding down Rayburn wrote this in his journal: "A very full day climaxed by a mess of a meeting with the hostesses that just left me worn out and sick. There is NO USE ever trying to get along with that outfit. Praise the Lord for at least keeping us sweet!" (Sublett, *The Diaries of Jim Rayburn*, 80).

46. Senter, *The Coming Revolution in Youth Ministry*, 44.

47. Shelley, *Helping Those Who Don't Want Help*, 59.

48. Hine, *Rise and Fall of the American Teenager*, 224.

were called to work in factories, leaving the child rearing and other duties to be done by their daughters. By 1947 Eugene Gilbert said, "Our salient discovery is that within the past decade teenagers have become a separate and distinct group in our society."[49] By the end of the war, with 80 percent of the teenage population enrolled in high school, advertisers were recognizing the potential of this new market. During the 1950s, teenagers spent 9.5 million dollars annually. By the 1960s, it skyrocketed to 12 billion dollars—more than 1000 times greater.[50] With millions of young people now searching for the "abundant life" it didn't take too long for American businesses to realize they had a new market. "[I]n 1944 *Seventeen*, the first magazine aimed specifically at this age group, was started. It defined, for the first time, a distinctive teenage market: millions of young people looking for acceptance, competency, fun, and sex, and, therefore, the right clothes, cosmetics, clear skin, great shoes, new music, and all the latest things."[51]

The process that Hall had begun over a half century earlier with these teenagers' grandparents was coming to its climax. From the start of the Great Depression to the end of the Second World War, the American family had witnessed a transformation in the very fabric of its makeup—adolescents were no longer children. They had a voice in family affairs and expected to enjoy a private social life. Now understood as "bobby soxers" and "teenagers," what had once been the privilege of the wealthy upper class was now part of the normal teenage life. Leading young people into the mysteries of adulthood was now the concern of educators, professional experts, and business leaders—all who had their own ideas of what was best for the emerging youth culture.[52]

An economic boom—and technological advances—also assisted in the creation of the teenage subculture. Most parents no longer needed their children to bring money into the household; quite the opposite, in fact, as parents either gave their children an allowance to spend however they wished or the teenagers took jobs and kept all the money they earned. The emergence from an all-consuming war also added to the mix of factors. Teenagers were in the mood to shop. During the war they had worked; they served in the armed forces, endured the loss of family and friends, and made do with very little as rations were meted out. With the war over,

---

49. Palladino, *Teenagers*, 110.
50. Schultze, *Dancing in the Dark*; Palladino, *Teenagers*.
51. Hine, *Rise and Fall of the American Teenager*, 232.
52. Palladino, *Teenagers*.

young people were eager to taste the fruits of their efforts and adult marketers were lining up to help them spend their new income.[53] This economic prosperity fueled new businesses, springing up to cater to this new market, which in turn reinforced the teenage subculture by either creating products the youth wanted or selling them on products they thought teenagers would want. But even the first marketers had misassumptions about what teenagers were all about. Some attempted to steer young people along a wholesome path—what they deemed building character—by attempting to shape teenage tastes along the lines of what adults found appropriate.[54] Palladino goes on to state:

> This certainly is not the image that pioneer marketers envisioned back in the 1940s, when they first began to promote teenagers as a group apart. On the contrary, they usually portrayed teenagers as fun-loving, wholesome high school students eager to try out adult freedoms, but willing to live by adult rules. In fact, when they referred to teenagers, they actually had adolescents in mind, a term that dated back to the nineteenth century. According to the experts—psychologists and educators who popularized the idea—adolescents were awkward, vulnerable creatures, the innocent victims of raging hormones, rampant insecurity, and fervent idealism (which often bordered on arrogance), characteristics that were apparently linked to puberty and a lack of experience. Because they were susceptible to worldly temptations (like cigarettes, dance halls, gambling, and liquor), adolescents had to be protected from the adult world, ideally in high school. There they could work through the storm and stress of their teenage years in a disciplined, wholesome, adult-guided environment. In the process, they would discover their talents and goals, develop good work habits, and learn the value of respect for authority—or so the theory went.[55]

It is interesting to note that marketers for profit-making businesses utilized similar theories about "character building" to sell their products as did the social reformers and religious organizations that were attempting to reach the youth. They, too, had bought into the concepts and theories of adolescence created decades before. Marketers, however, began to more specifically define the teenage market by creating "a new social type." By

---

53. Ibid.
54. Ibid.
55. Ibid., xv.

1941 marketers began to promote the "teenster," "teenager," or "bobby soxers" (whose only concern in life was to dance and have a good time) by tying them to the world of the high school. Dating, driving, and music were to be enjoyed by teenagers, but in a wholesome way as projected by adults. Students were supposed to be fun-loving conformists who only wanted to be part of the crowd.[56] But by 1950 the "revolution" in the approach to young people was nearly finished. Over the previous three decades almost every state "extended the legal protection by the juvenile court to those between 16 and 18 or 20. In effect, adolescence became a legal as well as a social category."[57]

The new evangelical parachurch ministries to young people were successful because they packaged Christianity in a popular manner and grew because of their appeal. Hart argues that although the impulse of fundamental or evangelical work in the early twentieth century might have been to protect young people from the hostile world that surrounded them, they were actually innovative in the manner in which they packaged their ministries. Once the fundamentalist/modernist controversy took place and evangelical organizations were forced to forge their own institutional bodies outside of denominational ties, parachurch ministries discovered the blend of what Hart describes as a "unique blend of gospel zeal and practical know-how, which in turn produced a subculture that was, to insiders, as fun-loving and vigorous."[58]

Utilizing the newfound independence and zeal for entertainment amongst young people was the Youth for Christ[59] movement. Youth for

56. Ibid.
57. Kett, *Rites of Passage*, 245.
58. Hart, *That Old-Time Religion*, 81–82.

59. Youth for Christ, officially organized in 1945, had various streams that led to its formation. Lloyd Bryant began attracting young people to Christ in the late 1920s and early 1930s through his radio broadcasts out of New York City. In the 1930s he toured the United States with a film titled *Youth Marches On* and created momentum for city-wide rallies for youth (Cannister, *Starting Right*). In the early years of Youth for Christ, rallies were drawing thousands of young people. In 1944 there were seventy thousand young people gathered at Chicago Stadium, thirty thousand gathered in 1946 at the state fair grounds for the second Youth for Christ convention, and in 1945 eighteen thousand young people gathered in Hollywood Bowl in Los Angeles for a rally (Larson, *Youth for Christ*). With rallies taking place across the United States and around the world, Youth for Christ chairman Torrey Johnson concluded in 1944 that they needed a full-time staff person to travel to rallies in order to speak at as many as possible. In later months of that year, Billy Graham was hired as the first full-time evangelist for Youth for Christ (Larson, *Youth for Christ*).

History

Christ was influential on the evangelical youth ministry landscape because they became skillful at using mass media for promotion and combined that with a civic devotion that showed other evangelicals how to garner the attention of the public as a whole.[60] In 1940 Jack Wyrtzen joined the scene when he formed a youth rally that was held on a Saturday nights in New York City. In connection to his radio program, the Word of Life Hour, Wyrtzen had growing success holding rallies in the city on the weekend and traveling with a gospel team to smaller towns during the week. In 1943 Wyrtzen was prompted to move his Saturday night rally from Carnegie Hall in New York to Madison Square Garden. Twenty thousand young people showed up for the rally, and they had to turn away another ten thousand because of capacity. With the success of this rally, news of the achievement of their evangelical outreach spread, and the foundation for Youth for Christ was set.[61] Youth for Christ led the way in this endeavor when Torrey Johnson[62] and Robert Cook wrote a book titled *Reaching Youth for Christ* (1945). This book contributed to the Youth for Christ momentum as leaders learned how to make faith relevant and upbeat to young people. Leaders in Youth for Christ, through their citywide rallies, came to understand that young people expected production levels that would rival Hollywood standards. Therefore, effective ministry to young people required the best comedy, great gospel music, and stirring testimonials. Without those elements young people would shun meetings that failed to meet these high standards. Though the pattern and formula for rallies might vary a little, meetings usually included good music, a testimony from a born-again young person, a God centered message, and all of this coordinated by a serviceman when possible.[63] Youth for Christ usually aimed for an informal atmosphere and liked to consider it a youth rally more than a church service.[64]

But Shelley believes that Young Life had a role in the emerging youth culture of the 1940s through language. He states,

> No one, however, made a more persistent attempt to understand the teenager than Jim Rayburn . . . He adopted the youth dialect of

---

60. Carpenter, *Revive Us Again*, 162.

61. Larson, *Youth for Christ*, 20.

62. Shelley states, "Torrey Johnson and his YFC colleagues designed their rallies to appeal to youth: the music, the personalities, the pace of the Saturday night meetings were all tailored to youth tastes" (Shelley, *Helping Those Who Don't Want Help*, 59).

63. Hart, *That Old-Time Religion*, 78–79.

64. Larson, *Youth for Christ*, 21.

the time. For example, "gang" and "swell"⁶⁵ are sprinkled throughout the early issues of Young Life. But more importantly he pursued the basic principles of communication in another culture like a foreign missionary.⁶⁶

As ministries such as Youth for Christ were utilizing the emerging teenage consumer culture, Young Life was marketing their ministry by speaking the language of young people. As Rayburn symbolizes through is colloquial use of "gang" and "swell," Young Life was making an effort not just to co-opt the emerging teenage culture of the 1940s but to identify with the young people they were working with through their communication style. As I will discuss in later chapters, language and communication style continues to shape the ministry of Young Life today.

Post-WWII Patriotic Fervor

As I have outlined, the trends of the fundamentalist/evangelical church and the golden era of teenagers had an impact on the foundation and characteristic of evangelical youth organizations of the early twentieth century. A third trend that influenced the foundation of evangelical youth ministries was the mood and culture in America during and after WWII. Evangelicals were no different than other Americans. Civic faith and faith in Christ blended with each other. This effect was heightened during the so-called American century when many thought that God's promise to the United States was being fulfilled. The country had played decisive roles in both world wars and had quickly thereafter become engaged in a struggle with "godless communism." "In America, and especially in revivalist traditions, the heart took sway over the head, and the heart is notoriously subject to the prevailing political winds. As Marsden concludes, fundamentalists and evangelicals drew deeply 'from the stockpile of American assumptions and concepts.'"⁶⁷

The Second World War shaped a generation as described by Mark Senter:

> The war created a crusade spirit. Young Americans who entered the war discovered their abilities to lead and drew on the resources

---

65. Attention will be given to this idea and to phrases such as these in following chapters.
66. Shelley, *Helping Those Who Don't Want Help*, 59.
67. Pahl, *Youth Ministry in Modern America*, 65.

of their homeland to rid the world of the fascist threat of Germany and imperialist ambitions of Japan. With victories on both fronts, American service personnel returned home convinced they had saved the world.[68] Soon Christian young adults were ready to participate in another crusade—a campaign to change the spiritual convictions of the nation and the world. The worldly wise young believers returned home to lead the church in cooperative efforts of evangelism.[69]

Youth for Christ began with revivals targeted at young people and not only urged a personal commitment to Christ but also encouraged the youth "to be patriotic Americans who lived lives of personal moral purity. Witnesses for Christ could also be warriors for the American way. Evangelical movements not only have been culturally confirming but also have linked personal conversion with efforts to reform American society."[70] Pahl argues that evangelical movements have been influential in linking personal conversion with reform in American society, and that Youth for Christ encouraged young people to be witnesses for purity and patriotism. Young people were encouraged within these emerging evangelical movements to become warriors for the American way.[71] Especially in light of the turmoil the world war brought to Americans at that time, witnesses for Christ were pressed into service.

> Dressing revivalism in more fashionable attire and merging it with Americans' growing concern for their fate in a troubled world, Youth for Christ pioneered a new evangelical outreach. The rallies blended fundamentalists and other evangelicals into a broad coalition and showed how the movement might win a valued place once more in the public life of the nation.[72]

---

68. One Young Life person who would eventually become president of the organization was impacted by his time serving in the Navy. Young Life historian Char Meredith states, "One of the young officers who came out of the Navy after the war enrolled at Wheaton College in Illinois. With the scars of violence and killing gouged in his mind, Bill Starr returned to his education with a strong conviction: only a living out of the life of Jesus Christ could prevent a third world war from demolishing the earth" (Meredith, *It's a Sin to Bore a Kid*, 52).

69. Senter, *The Coming Revolution in Youth Ministry*, 109.

70. Pahl, *Youth Ministry in Modern America*, 6.

71. Ibid.

72. Carpenter, *Revive Us Again*, 162.

In his role as Youth for Christ evangelist, Billy Graham played to this fearful/hopeful perspective:

> Much of Graham's message sounded like America was more Babylon than Israel. He tied anxieties about the threat of nuclear destruction with Biblical warnings of judgment for sin. He preached for conversions and for traditional American values. Though he stayed away from public involvement in politics, he spoke often of the communist threat and the dangers to America of such atheistic and materialistic values.[73]

Creating a crusade paradigm allowed revivalist and fundamentalist preachers to both condemn the current state of the nation and to inspire young adults to step up and fight for good against the evils all around them. The urgency of the fight (especially during the Second World War), the immediacy of its impact, the valor of the military hero, the grandeur of the military machine—all of these images were utilized to inspire both faith in Christ and commitment to the country. "In all Youth for Christ assemblies, the war is presented as a holy crusade, the service of Christ and the military service of country are equated, and soldiers, sailors, marines and members of the women's auxiliaries are singled out for special honor . . . in a 'smooth blend of religion and patriotism.'"[74]

Carpenter credits the rapid success of Youth for Christ to the growing number of evangelicals at the time and the restyling of revivals into the skillful promotion of rallies that rivaled Hollywood entertainment at the time. But Carpenter also notes that external factors must have played a part as well. What he calls the "Spirit of Pearl Harbor," the years of World War II acted not only as a tonic for Americans' faith but also brought to light the nations ideals. The war years brought with it prosperity, mobility, and a regeneration of Americans' civic faith.[75]

"Anticommunism was America's consensus ideology during the Cold War, and while it exaggerated nuclear anxieties, it also provided Americans with enemies within and without to contend against."[76] To effectively fight against the godless communists, one first had to make a dual commitment: to Christ and to the Christian nation of the United States. Youth for Christ (and Young Life, as will be shown in following chapters) seized upon this

---

73. Marsden, *Religion and American Culture*, 217.
74. Pahl, *Youth Ministry in Modern America*, 59.
75. Carpenter, *Revive Us Again*, 167.
76. Pahl, *Youth Ministry in Modern America*, 122.

battle and used it for their own ends. As had been done over centuries, religious organizations supported the state while the state served to support the religious organizations—one culture, under God.

Jim Rayburn: Pioneer[77] of Young Life

Andrew Root states that as the parachurch movement expanded within the United States from 1940 to 1960 he believes the model of relational youth ministry was unleashed. The Young Life organization was adding its distinct mark to the youth parachurch movement within the United States in the early 1940s, including this new attitude towards relationships as argued by Root. However, the emergence of Young Life as a youth movement has as much to do with the influence of its founder as it does with the state of the evangelical church at the time. The history of the organization begins with the fundamental upbringing of founder Jim Rayburn and his formation growing up within an evangelical family. Root argues that Rayburn and the Young Life organization "invented" this form of youth ministry. Though not alone in their work during this period, Root believes Youth for Christ was confronting a major shift in American culture as well as addressing the distinct youth culture that was forming, while Young Life addressed a new form and attitude towards relationships within society. Comparing the two organizations, Root states, "Both organizations in their own ways confronted the two major shifts occurring within the broader American culture: the arrival of a distinct youth culture was most prominently addressed by Youth for Christ,[78] and Young Life focused on the new attitude

---

77. The term "pioneer" was used by Rayburn himself. In his Chicago Fellowship address to church leaders he states, "We are stirred by this call to pioneer a frontier movement . . . .We simply must let God make us frontiersmen . . . .This is the spirit in which we must go. We simply must let God make us frontiersmen—frontiersmen of a big, new, daring plan that we can implement" (Rayburn, Chicago Fellowship transcript). The Chicago Fellowship was a gathering of Christian leaders from across the country to hear Rayburn speak on the efforts and strategy of the Young Life movement. Bill Starr stated, "I think it was Jim's way of asking for acceptance, but it was also to help churchmen understand that Young Life was a useful tool, an authentic way to help them get the gospel out" (Meredith, *It's a Sin to Bore a Kid*). Starr also stated this about the "pioneer" spirit of Young Life: "Our founders from the very beginning were pioneer spirits who recognized a couple things about the young world of the adolescent: teenagers desire to move out beyond the familiar, and teenagers like to be led" (Young Life, *Focus on Youth*, Winter 1975, 3).

78. In the following chapter I will outline the ways in which Young Life also addresses

toward relationships within society that was allowing for greater choice in the realms of friendship, sexuality, and intimacy."[79]

The Early Days of Rayburn

Rayburn was born in the early 1900s in Newton, Kansas. Born into a family of Presbyterians, Rayburn's father worked as a traveling evangelist for the church in the southwest, and Jim would often travel with him on these tours playing cornet and singing in the choir. On these evangelistic tours, Jim would often hear about the evils of drinking, card playing, and dancing.[80] His life was dictated by the conservative and fundamental upbringing his parents adhered to: Sunday was the Sabbath day, and the only book you could read on that day was the Bible, no game playing on the Sabbath including baseball, and there was no running, shouting or hitting allowed. Rayburn's mom was likened to a Christian Marine Corps recruiter who ran her household with strictness and efficiency.[81]

Rayburn graduated from Kansas State University with a degree in geology, but after graduation and his marriage to wife Maxine, job prospects were limited. When the Presbyterian Church offered him a position as a missionary pastor in small churches in the southwest, he jumped at the chance.[82] He was given the task of establishing a ministry to young people in the community and made this statement about Sunday school: "If you want anybody to show up, don't have it on Sunday and don't call it school."[83] Jim and Maxine Rayburn moved to Clifton, Arizona, and it was here that Rayburn had a life changing experience. While ministering in Clifton, Rayburn began to wonder how much he was missing in terms of the meaning of the gospel. He was preaching what he had heard his father preach—restrictions and condemnation of sins. Dealing in these clichés was not satisfying his spiritual hunger, nor did it go a great distance in reaching the young people

---

the emerging youth culture of the 1940s through attracting young people to Christ through images, language, and a style of outreach that they felt worked most efficiently for their ministry, therefore I disagree with Root that Youth for Christ had the corner on the distinct youth culture.

79. Root, *Revisiting Relational Youth Ministry*, 49.
80. Meredith, *It's a Sin to Bore a Kid*, 12.
81. Rayburn III, *Dance, Children, Dance*.
82. Ibid.
83. Ibid., 27.

of these communities. During this period Rayburn concluded "it was a sin to bore kids with the gospel."[84]

While staying at one of the parsonages in Clifton, Rayburn found a book written by Lewis Sperry Chafer[85] titled *He That is Spiritual* and was finally able to connect the joy of salvation by grace alone. Rayburn stated, "I was a gospel preacher, I led people to the Lord Jesus Christ, I was a member of the Board of National Missions of the Presbyterian Church, if you please, before I ever heard of this—the absolute finality and perfection of what Jesus Christ has done about sin."[86]

In a section discussing "grace-truth," Chafer states,

> True spirituality is a divine output of the life, rather than a mere cessation of the things which are called "worldly." It does not consist in what one does not do; it is rather what one does. It is not suppression; it is expression. It is not holding in self; it is living out Christ. . . . Worldly Christians turn to so-called worldly things because they discover in them an anesthetic to deaden the pain of an empty heart and life. . . . The cure is to fill the heart and life with

---

84. Meredith, *It's a Sin to Bore a Kid*. This, then, becomes a marker that will set Young Life apart from other youth organizations like Youth for Christ—which held more firmly to a traditional fundamentalist outlook. In a reflection from a former YFC student he believed the presentation of the "good news" was far from it. "The solution to the predicament [of sin], as I understood it, was not to rely utterly on the grace of God . . . rather, the way of salvation seemed to lay in subscribing to a set of doctrines and then hewing to strict standards of morality, usually expressed in negative terms: don't dance, drink, smoke, swear or attend movies" (Pahl, *Youth Ministry in Modern America*, 68).

85. "A native of Ohio and a Congregationalist minister, Chafer's religious roots were firmly planted in the kind of devotion that Dwight L. Moody, revivalist extraordinary, had popularized during the last decades of the nineteenth century. Chafer was committed to winning new converts and improving believers' understanding of the Bible . . . . In 1922 he moved to Dallas, Texas, and two years later founded Dallas Theological Seminary, the intellectual headquarters for dispensationalism" (Hart, *That Old-Time Religion*, 34).

86. Rayburn III, *Dance, Children, Dance*, 31–32. This finality of sin as perfected by Jesus was a stream that historically ran through evangelicalism. "According to H.K. Carroll, writing in 1893, the beliefs that united all Protestants under the umbrella of evangelicalism were the 'inspiration, authority and sufficiency' of the Bible, the Trinity, the deity of Christ, justification 'by faith alone,' and the work of the Holy Spirit 'in the conversion and sanctification of the sinner.' Twentieth-century evangelicals such as Riley, Chafer, Bryan, Rimmer and Price would have had no trouble agreeing with any part of these doctrinal platforms'" (Hart, *That Old-Time Religion*, 45).

the eternal blessing of God.[87] We have a message of the imperishable Spring. It is the outflow of the limitless life of God.[88]

However, Rayburn's relationship with the organized church was tenuous at times. Meredith states, "During the early '30s, Jim's own active rebellion against traditional religious structures laid the foundation for his effectiveness with kids."[89] Rayburn noted in a journal that after sitting in a meeting for the church synod that he found it a perfect bore and would regret it the rest of his life.[90] But from his reading of Chafer and his change in understanding about the purpose of the Christian life, Rayburn felt led to attend the seminary that Chafer founded, Dallas Theological Seminary[91] in Texas.

Rayburn's connection to, and transformation by, Lewis Sperry Chafer cannot be taken too lightly. Chafer was a leading theologian in the arena of dispensationalism in the early 1900s. Hart argues that Chafer was one of the prominent popularizers of this type of biblical interpretation that would come to dominate twentieth-century evangelicalism and could be considered an institution builder because of it. Because of his popularity in dispensationalism, Chafer was often invited to be a speaker at conferences around the world. Chafer was a speaker at one of the first World Christian Fundamentals' Association conference and was considered a "rarely gifted Bible teacher."[92] Chafer, having established Dallas Seminary

---

87. To highlight the extent to which Rayburn gravitated to this epiphany we see his complaint of lack of spiritual blessing in his journal entry from Monday, February 22, 1943: "Just too pooped to do any good. Then on top of all of that I am all flustered about staff problems—this will be remembered as the day I pulled one of the biggest boneheads of my life—and manifested that I have not been letting the Holy Spirit fill me and empower me!" (Sublett, *The Diaries of Jim Rayburn*, 116).

88. Chafer, *He That Is Spiritual*, 82.

89. Meredith, *It's a Sin to Bore a Kid*, 15.

90. Ibid; Rayburn III, *Dance, Children, Dance*.

91. "Even so, during the first half of the twentieth century, theological education at places such as Dallas and Westminster reinforced evangelical zeal for the Bible as the fountain of all truth and hope. As already observed, under Chafer's leadership Dallas emerged as the intellectual center of dispensationalism. At first the school sought to train pastors primarily for the southern Presbyterian Church (PCUS). But after an investigation by the denomination severed informal ties to the seminary, Dallas's faculty and students came from and returned to nondenominational network of churches and schools that had grown up around the Bible prophecy conference movement of the late nineteenth century" (Hart, *That Old-Time Religion*, 51).

92. Hart, *That Old-Time Religion*, 34.

in 1924, was invited to be a speaker at the Keswick Convention,[93] a conference that maintained close links between British conservative evangelicals and American fundamentals.

Hart argues that one influence of the Keswick convention can be linked with the writings of Chafer. He highlights the work of Chafer that notes evangelicals should be people of the book [Bible] yet could offer few specifics from that book on how people should live. "[Chafer] wrote, "A Spiritual Christian is a Spirit-filled Christian in whom the unhindered Spirit is manifesting Christ by producing a true Christian character, which is the fruit of the spirit. How misleading, is the theory that to be spiritual one must abandon play, diversion and helpful amusement."[94] The Christian life, then, for Chafer, was one filled with the divine love of God and one not based on the rules and regulations often found in fundamental and evangelical circles. The first move as a godly Christian was to be filled with God's presence, and from there, life would be centered on service and yielded to the will of God. I believe part of the transforming power of Chafer on the life of Jim Rayburn was the permission given to embrace the playfulness and amusement of Christian life. By embracing the writings of Chafer, Rayburn was able to shed his fundamental and restrictive upbringing and focus his work and the Young Life organization on the divine fulfillment of God's spirit through play, diversion or helpful amusement.

Rayburn had this to say about Chafer: "So far as I am concerned, personally, there would have been no Young Life work at all without Dr. Lewis Chafer's course in soteriology."[95] Rayburn concluded that his entire life had changed when he discovered, through the work of Chafer, that the Holy Spirit could be considered a real person—doing things in his life that could only be done by God. He encouraged others to bow down to the influences of the Spirit and to open their lives to Jesus Christ as the Spirit prompted them to do.[96] However, as far as I can conclude from my research, Rayburn did not carry Chafer's dispensational influence of theology into the work of

---

93. Marsden notes that the Keswick Convention, first started in 1875 in connection with the revivals of Moody, was an informal meeting place for British conservative evangelicals. The emphasis on "Bible study, evangelism, missions, personal piety and victory over sin" had a wide influence on those who participated (Marsden, "Fundamentalism," 308).

94. Hart, *That Old-Time Religion*, 75.

95. Rayburn III, *Dance, Children, Dance*, 132.

96. Ibid.

Young Life. The main influence does seem to be in the area of salvation and the joyous life that comes with it.

Char Meredith highlights the spiritual discipline of play and amusement that influenced Rayburn through Chafer, noting it was Rayburn's personality[97] that made Young Life popular in the early days. Rayburn was bold and adventurous and would go to great lengths to tell kids about Christ. He would pile kids into his Jeep and head into the mountains to go snow jumping. Wally Howard summed up Rayburn's style by stating, "His faith had a daredevil quality about it. There were times when I could not decide if he was a man of God or just presumptuous, whether he was driven by ambition to serve Christ or to build his own empire."[98] His charismatic style of speaking attracted thousands of people from young to old. He crisscrossed the country in the early years speaking to groups or individuals, leading school assemblies, preaching in churches, and meeting with whomever would listen to him about Young Life. Rayburn concluded that young people were not ignoring the church because of the message of Jesus Christ—they were ignoring the church because of the stifled feeling of the whole ecclesiastical system. Rayburn would come to be known for the phrase, "It's a sin to bore a kid."[99] Rayburn, during a training session, stated, "When you talk to kids about the sovereign of all that is, the One who made you and everything else, the One who became one of us, the One who died for us, and the One who is alive for us today—DON'T YOU DARE BORE ANYONE WITH THAT. If you can't do this, then you need to get better acquainted with the One you're talking about."[100]

Early Days of Young Life

While at Dallas Seminary, Rayburn had a part time job working in a church in Gainesville, Texas. Clyde Kennedy, the senior pastor, came up with a

---

97. "This expansion of evangelical Christianity did not proceed primarily from the nimble response of religious elites meeting the challenge before them. Rather, Christianity was effectively reshaped by common people who molded it in their own image and threw themselves into expanding its influence. Increasingly assertive common people wanted their leaders unpretentious, their doctrines self-evident and down-to-earth, their music lively and singable, and their churches in local hands" (Hatch, *The Democratization of American Christianity*, 9).

98. Rayburn III, *Dance, Children, Dance*, 83.

99. Meredith, *It's a Sin to Bore a Kid*.

100. Miller, *Back to the Basics*, 61. Capitals in original.

novel idea: Rayburn, who was in charge of youth ministries, would work exclusively with un-churched kids. Adopting the name of an already established ministry to high school students, Rayburn began his Miracle Book Club and started working with local high school students. It was slow going at first for Rayburn. "If you want to see a bunch of sad apples, just have a meeting for the kids who'll stay after school. I got the biggest selection of teachers' pets you ever saw, not a red corpuscle in the whole crowd. Everybody I wanted to reach was out on the football field, and everyplace else, right while we were having our club meeting. After nine months of that, I knew I had to try something else." During the school year of 1940, Rayburn changed the name from Miracle Book Club to Young Life Campaign,[101] and the eventual international ministry began.[102]

Jim Rayburn III gives account of the first days of Young Life. The first meetings, in the summer of 1940, were evangelistic crusades complete with a choir, quartet, and preaching. There was even a children's meeting. During that summer, Rayburn, using a conversational style of communication, spoke to more than 13,000 people in his canvas church. "No longer associated with the Miracle Book Club, the leaders were considering what to call themselves during the summer tent campaigns coming up. . . . Young Life Campaign appealed to them more than any other. . . . 'We rather liked the aggressive feel of the word campaign.'"[103] One memory from this summer evangelistic outreach was the style Rayburn utilized. "Jim did things on the platform in such a funny way. He was a great joke teller, a master at getting people's attention, hamming up a Bible story to make it live. 'Do you stop having fun when you start talking about Jesus? If you do, God help you.'"[104] "Along with his seminary buddies Addison Sewell and Walden Howard, he sought ways to build a bridge to teenagers in the area around Dallas. Across from the fair park some businessmen helped them put up a tent with a 'God Bless America'[105] banner. It was a start. The Christian faith is what

---

101. In 1937 Frederick Wood, founder of the Young Life Campaign in Britain, accepted an invitation of Lloyd Bryant to speak at rallies for young people in the United States. While in Texas, Wood had the opportunity to meet Jim Rayburn, and Rayburn received the blessing of Wood to use the name of Young Life in the US (Cannister, *Starting Right*).

102. Rayburn III, *Dance, Children, Dance*, 44.

103. Meredith, *It's a Sin to Bore a Kid*, 24.

104. Ibid., 19.

105. "By the time the first regional conferences were held in late 1944, evangelicals (mostly fundamentalists) in several major cities had already initiated campaigns under

made America strong, they reasoned. A kid can't be a good American if he doesn't understand that faith."[106] From this summer tent experience and through his contacts with fellow pastors at the seminary, Rayburn managed to recruit sixty-five volunteers to begin working with high school students through his Young Life Campaign. That fall, they began working in Dallas, Gainesville, and Houston, Texas, and Young Life was on its way.[107]

Lewis Sperry Chafer invited Rayburn to address the Dallas Theological Seminary chapel about his campaign.[108] Through this address and the seminary students that had volunteered to assist, Rayburn and his new campaign began to reach young people. Rayburn would teach the volunteers on Wednesday afternoons on his new emerging Young Life method of evangelism. In the early days these methods were discovered as important: don't hold a club after school if you want kids to do what they like to do, evening is a better time to meet, kids will go where their friends are so attract leaders of the school, and kids are more comfortable in an informal setting rather than church or school.[109] By December 1940, Rayburn had officially organized the Young Life Campaign with a board of directors.

Ted Benson and his wife Mary Lou were also students at the seminary at the time of Rayburn and were influential in making a vital connection for Rayburn in the early days of Young Life. Benson had come from Chicago and had worked with the Christian Workers' Foundation. This foundation had been organized by Herbert J. Taylor,[110] president of Club Aluminum,

---

the sponsorship 'Christ for America,' an initiative launched by Horace F. Dean, vice president of the Philadelphia Bible School. Its inspiration came from a revival campaign held in Philadelphia during 1942, sponsored by the Philadelphia Fundamentalist Association and featuring Hyman Appelman, an evangelist from Texas" (Carpenter, *Revive Us Again*, 159).

106. Meredith, *It's a Sin to Bore a Kid*, 18.

107. Rayburn III, *Dance, Children, Dance*.

108. Chafer would continue to provide opportunities for Rayburn beyond Rayburn's graduation from the seminary. In a letter written to a friend Chafer states, "Rayburn is almost supernatural in his appeal and power with these young people . . . Follow his instructions and you will see miracles on a very large scale on a most blessedly true Gospel foundation" (Sublett, *The Diaries of Jim Rayburn*, 141).

109. Meredith, *It's a Sin to Bore a Kid*.

110. Taylor formed the Christian Workers Foundation by giving twenty-five percent of his Club Aluminum stock to the foundation. The purpose of the foundation was to reach un-churched young people across America that included evangelistic works aimed at college students down through high school students and elementary kids. He stated, "With God's help . . . we intended to help pioneer and finance the non-denominational organizations we felt would do the best job of reaching these young people with the

who also was heavily invested financially with InterVarsity Christian Fellowship and Child Evangelism. Taylor was on the lookout for an organization that worked with high school students. Benson wrote in a letter to him, "This fellow Jim Rayburn here has some different ideas on how to reach high school kids. You might want to talk to him."[111] As Young Life grew in the early years, Rayburn held the position as chief spokesperson for the organization as well as chief fundraiser. Relying on a nucleus of friends across the country, Rayburn was in charge of raising all of the funds for the organization as well as staff people across the country. There were often times when staff would rely on the provision of God and pray for miracles in order to make budget for certain months. The same would be true, in coming years, for the blossoming camping ministry that Young Life would embark upon.[112]

John Miller, a long time staff person for Young Life noted the evolution of the Young Life campaign in the early days from the early tent meetings to the eventual club methodology that would become one of the key components of the Young Life ministry:

> [Rayburn] tried a tent meeting. He tried a school meeting. He tried a church meeting. He then decided to try a meeting in the home of one of the kids on a school night. A dramatic change! The first Young Life club in the history of the world came alive and grew rapidly to 100, 125, 150 kids. Why? Because a good fisherman kept asking himself what were they biting on and to what would kids respond. He refused to keep using bait that didn't work.[113]

In the early days of ministerial discovery for the Young Life organization it, then, became a distancing by Rayburn from other ministry models that surrounded him. He discarded the evangelical tent meetings of his father, the student led Miracle Book Club meetings, and at the same time distanced his ministry from the mass rally model of Youth for Christ. Relational, incarnational[114] ministry became the pragmatic tool utilized by Young Life to present the gospel to young people in the United States.

Lord's word" (Shelley, *Fides et Historia*, 47). Taylor would play a key role in Young Life in the early days from mentoring Jim Rayburn to purchasing the first property for Young Life camp in Colorado and leasing the camp to Young Life for $1 a year (Rayburn III, *Dance, Children, Dance*).

111. Meredith, *It's a Sin to Bore a Kid*, 19.

112. Miller, *Back to the Basics of Young Life*.

113. Ibid., 54.

114. As described in the introduction to this thesis, the term incarnational describes

Trial and Error

The same foundation is echoed in an informational booklet produced by Young Life in 1965.[115] Reflecting the life of founder Jim Rayburn, it noted the talent, energy, and faith Rayburn had and his passion to "muster an all-out effort to gain interest and enthusiasm in the high school set."[116] It continues by stating, "Rayburn had no program to follow; but it appeared to him that the club idea was a valid vehicle, simply because high school kids like nothing better than being together with their friends. . . . By attitude, word, deed he seemed to be communicating the hero of the Bible was a real man, as well as God—the only Person who would ever deserve their highest admiration and allegiance. He used no gimmicks. He held out genuine friendship to the kids, and a message that glowed with the winsome figure of Jesus Christ."[117] From the beginning, Young Life was seeking new routes to the high school crowd: "keeping what seemed workable, throwing out what failed."[118]

In this same information booklet, Young Life itself titles this process of figuring out a way to relate with adolescents as "trial and error." It states that as the Young Life ministry idea caught in community after community, leaders felt their way according to their skills. "Some ideas flopped," and then they go on to say, "some were so successful they became an integral part of the Young Life concept, which had spread by this time into several states."[119] But as Young Life grew as an organization, their leaders felt it was important to train their staff. The process of trial and error became tedious to Rayburn and his staff, so it was decided that a training school would be set up for leaders. Professors who were in "harmony with Young Life objectives" were contacted to provide training for staff people. "The first year the Young Life 'students' traveled by station wagon to 'sit at their professor's feet' on a number of different campuses."[120]

---

the method of ministry that follows the pattern of Jesus who is believed to be the human incarnate of God. Young Life leaders operate as servants of Christ as human witnesses that incarnate the life of Christ. I will discuss in depth the relational, incarnational foundation and emphasis of Young Life in the following chapter.

115. Field Journal, May 2008.
116. Young Life, informational booklet, 21.
117. Ibid., 23.
118. Ibid.
119. Ibid., 25.
120. Ibid., 27.

History

According to Mark Senter, this high school club methodology was forged by Jim Rayburn and perfected within Young Life in the 1940s and 1950s. A similar strategy was then adopted by Youth for Christ in the 1960s[121] and had continued traction within ecclesial youth ministries in the 1970s. Senter states, "Rayburn's contribution was at the heart of the parachurch contribution to church youth ministry."[122] Based on their approach to working with young people, Young Life has had a significant impact on youth ministry in the United States. Since the ministry began with un-churched young people, Rayburn founded his work on "meeting kids where they're at." This style of ministry—relational and incarnational—has been the foundation for Young Life's work with young people over the decades.

In a leadership training manual Young Life states, "Jim Rayburn used to say, 'The best Young Life work is yet to be done.' The giants of Young Life's past have written important chapters in our mission's history, but our call remains constant and current—the needs of kids today are more urgent than ever. As you begin your ministry with Young Life you become another chapter in our history. How would you like your chapter to read?"[123] In relationship to shaping Young Life club in a manner that would best suit the needs of young people in a specific area, they suggest answering questions of God and the community. "Have we [the Young Life community] come to a consensus that God is leading us in a different direction regarding club? If so, in what way are we going to verbally proclaim the Gospel?"[124] Young Life provides room for flexibility within the organization and seeks to understand how that would affect the proclamation of the gospel. However, as noted above, Young Life did not provide as much flexibility in the specific case of Jeff McSwain and his staff in North Carolina. Young Life concludes their section on "tipping sacred cows" by stating,

> Jim Rayburn was an expert cow-tipper. He turned "Christian camping" on its head and took the gospel outside the walls of church to kids on campus. Yet it has been rightly said that the best Young Life work is yet to be done. To move effectively forward in the future means asking hard questions, then doing what works

---

121. Youth for Christ Bible clubs (called Campus Life) since 1960 have become the basic ministry units of YFC. They sponsor club meetings once a week with the intention of forming spirituality (Pahl, *Youth Ministry in Modern America*).

122. Senter, *The Coming Revolution in Youth Ministry*, 125.

123. Young Life, leadership training manual, 13.

124. Ibid., 132.

and doing it well. And sometimes it might mean following in the founder's footsteps and tipping a sacred cow.[125]

Rayburn's influence on youth ministry cannot be understated. He pioneered the leader-centered style of ministry—moving away from his original peer-oriented ministry within the Miracle Book Club. Andrew Root believes that incarnational ministry like that of Young Life "has been formed from the material of cultural engagement rather than from the theological pillars of the work of the incarnate Christ in the world."[126] Rayburn understood the leader to be the primary speaker responsible for communicating the message of Christ. Another contribution of Young Life is the philosophy of "winning the right to be heard" meaning leaders need to gain the respect of students before expecting them to listen to claims of Christ. "This had to be done on the young person's turf—football games and practices, high schoolers' hangouts such as soda fountains, school events, and when permitted by school authorities, the high school cafeteria. This whole process, which came to be known as 'incarnational theology' led to a point at which the Christian Gospel was presented."[127] John Miller illustrates this understanding: "Go where they are; seek them. We are God's seekers; people who look for those who are hiding. We go to their turf as He came to ours. Contact work is so clearly spiritual, so wonderfully Christlike. Do not ever underestimate the value and importance of your contact ministry. It is the very backbone of Young Life."[128]

THE 4 C'S

Though Miller argues at one point that contact work, or incarnational ministry, was the backbone of Young Life, he also notes the emphasis Rayburn and Young Life placed on the emerging camping ministry. This parallel evolution led Rayburn and Young Life to shape their ministry around weekly camps full of rides, adventures, entertainment, and the Gospel. John Miller stated, "The reason we have beautiful and well-equipped camps is to proclaim the gospel of Jesus Christ in a setting that speaks well of Him. The reason we provide campers with good food, good housing, excellent

125. Ibid., 133.
126. Root, *Revisiting Relational Youth Ministry*, 17.
127. Senter, *The Coming Revolution in Youth Ministry*, 126.
128. Miller, *Back to the Basics*, 98.

swimming pools, good ropes courses, fun water programs, Hondas and exceptional entertainment is to build an attractive platform from which we proclaim our message."[129]

Senter also agrees it was the camping ministry that set Young Life apart from other evangelical parachurch organizations within the United States:

> Rayburn had an instinct for ministry that others saw as folly. The purchase of Star Ranch near Colorado Springs in late 1945 seemed absurd to the Young Life board members since the organization had been unable to pay staff salaries and had ended the fiscal year in the black only as a result of a last-minute gift of $2,500 from board chairman, Herbert J. Taylor. The idea of investing $50,000 they certainly did not have into a camp they really did not need and then banking on attracting students from as far away as Texas, New York, and Bellingham, Washington, to that camp in Colorado seemed like a fantasy.[130]

The four methodologies, then, that emerged in the 1940s and 1950s of Young Life were: the weekly meeting of club, camp, the Bible study known as Campaigners, and contact work. In coming years, emerging in the 1960s, a fifth tenet, committee work, would be added when local groups of supportive adults would take over fundraising work and promotion of the Young Life ministry.

Young Life was attempting to articulate the power of their promise, "or what some experts call our 'brand strength.'"[131] The research process included internal research as well as work with a consultancy group. They conducted interviews with students, donors, and leaders, as well as those who support Young Life at the community level. This is the response they received: "[Young Life] heard that it is more than superficially fun. It is 'joy and a freedom to be who we are.' It is also 'someone's really crowded basement, a wall with song lyrics projected on it and my leader being really sweaty.'[132] Sweaty fun and sacrificial love—that sounds about right."[133] This

---

129. Ibid., 141.

130. Senter, *Coming Revolution in Youth Ministry*, 73–74.

131. *Relationships*, Spring 2007, 6.

132. Rick Yates expands on the idea of leadership within Young Life. "I do believe one of the important jobs of a leader is to find the funny people around him or her and utilize their gifts of humor. We need to recruit funny people and get them in front of kids" (Yates, *Skits for Camp*, 4).

133. *Relationships*, Spring 2007, 6.

statement of Young Life—what they claim as their "promise"—reiterates what they understand they are: they are about fun and love. They follow up by saying, "Young Life has a decades-long history of honoring its promise. What is essential about Young Life hasn't changed in more than 66 years. The consistency and power of Young Life's 'basics' are a God-given treasure that deserves intentional study and stewardship to keep it strong and extend its reach in a global community in 2008 and beyond. At its core, Young Life is Christ and kids."[134]

Primitivism

For Rayburn and the Young Life organization, there has always been tension between their work in presenting young people with the message of Jesus Christ and the relationship with the institutional church.[135] Rayburn, and in conjunction Young Life, were both striving for a purer understanding of religion, common in many revivalist movements, known as primitivism. Carpenter states, "Primitivism involves the tendency to blur the distinctions and distance between one's own time and an ideal past. Christian primitivism, according to historian Grant Wacker, refers to the 'yearning for pure doctrines, pure beginnings, and pure fulfillments' that only a recovery of the fresh and unspoiled or 'primitive' Christianity of the New Testament churches could bring."[136] To strive, as Rayburn illustrates, to live as a "New Testament Christian" was the ideal form of Christianity. Rayburn stated:

> I am identified with the modern institutional church. I am a member of one of the most institutional of them all, a Presbyterian minister in good standing in my presbytery for twenty-one years. Quite a record for a fellow in my line of work. The Presbyterians frown on anything they can't control, and I'll give you a clue: they can't control me. I am identified, and I trust loyally so and constructively so, with the local, organized church. But I am also engaged in the sincere attempt to get back to what New Testament Christianity was really all about. The heart and center of it was Jesus Christ and people.[137]

134. Ibid., 6.

135. I will discuss the relationship between the Church and Young Life in the following chapter.

136. Carpenter, *Revive Us Again*, 69.

137. Rayburn III, *Dance, Children, Dance*, 137.

For Emile Caillet, theologian from Princeton Seminary, observation of this thrust was apparent in Rayburn as well. "For Jim, the recovery of this New Testament outlook was at hand. He was led to acknowledge as his key Bible verse Colossians 4:5, 'Walk in wisdom toward them that are without . . .' He could hardly have foreseen the amount of exertion and trial and error implied in working out the wisdom mentioned in this New Testament passage."[138] John Miller states, "As I have grown in my understanding of Scripture and weighed Young Life in the light of Scripture, I've become increasingly convinced that Jim Rayburn has a unique and significant place in the entire Christian movement. The ministry he founded is so clearly rooted in Scripture—is so Christ-like in the manner in which it approaches teenagers and penetrates the teenage culture."[139]

Though Rayburn pioneered the Young Life organization in the United States, and heavily influenced the club and camping methodology for high school students, in 1964 the bottom fell out from under him. Struggling with addiction to pain killers for a stomach ailment and sleeping pills that would help him rest, Rayburn slurred his way through speaking engagements, or in one case, could not speak at all. The Young Life board was nervous Rayburn was casting a dubious light on the ministry as a whole, and asked him to step down as executive director. This caught Rayburn off guard at their May meeting, and he proceeded to schedule an appointment with a psychiatrist for a consultation. This medical report, shared with the board in June at another meeting, was ignored and Rayburn was, in all purposes, finished with Young Life as a ministry. There were other issues that Rayburn and his board disagreed on: management of money and staff, leadership and management of personnel, and the addition of camp property throughout the United States. In his lifetime, Rayburn had gangrene from a ruptured appendix, killed a man in a car accident, was struck by lightning, had chronic migraines, had stomach cancer and thus became addicted to pills for pain and sleeping. In the midst of this, his wife was also addicted to pain medication for chronic pain in her back and legs, and they no longer expressed love towards one another in a physical way. Six years after being asked to step down from leadership in the organization he helped form, Rayburn died.[140]

---

138. Cailliet, *Young Life*, 12.
139. Miller, *Back to the Basics*, 37.
140. Rayburn III, *Dance, Children, Dance*.

Though Rayburn was the pioneering charismatic leader that founded the Young Life ministry to young people in the United States, he also recruited a team of leaders and volunteers with his same vision of reaching high school students with the good news of Jesus who had previously been unreached with the message of Christ. Because of the recruitment of leaders and the expansion of ministry across the country, the Young Life organization transitioned through the change of leadership after Rayburn stepped down rather successfully. Bill Starr was named president of the ministry directly after Rayburn left, and led Young Life in that position for the next thirteen years.

In the following section I will show the formation and expansion of the Young Life organization in a general and descriptive way, covering the statistics of ministry, the characteristics of the organization, camping ministry, and the state of Young Life today.

Statistics of the Young Life Ministry: Formation to Expansion

As I have presented, the influences that formed the life of Jim Rayburn also shaped the Young Life organization. It is important to recognize that the organization was able to grow and flourish under numerous leaders and personnel over the years.[141] From staff to volunteers, from camping to club, the Young Life organization formed and expanded to what it is today. In this section I review pertinent information regarding the growth of staff and volunteers and their work of contact with students, the ministry of club and camping, and the expansion of the ministry across the United States. Through the foundation Rayburn laid in club methodology and interest in camping, Young Life was set on a trajectory that guides them today. Young Life often refers to their work as the 5 C's: Club, Camp, Campaigners, Contact Work, and Committee. This section will look at how these factors are manifest in later years, transitioning beyond the leadership of Rayburn.

---

141. In the preface to Rayburn's diaries, Kit Sublett stated that Rayburn believed in keeping statistics but warned about putting too much emphasis on them. Rayburn states, "We're never going to justify Young Life with numbers because our count may not match heaven's" (Sublett, *The Diaries of Jim Rayburn*, xx).

Staff, Volunteers, and Students

From the early days, Rayburn had access to a core of volunteers through his relationships with other seminary students at Dallas Theological Seminary. Dr. Chafer invited Rayburn to address the seminary, and from that encounter a regular class of forty students would meet with Rayburn on Wednesday afternoons. Out of that class, a number of them became the first wave of Young Life staff people and volunteers. As Rayburn experimented with his club methodology, he would call his classmates together after each club and inform them of what worked and what didn't. They would spend hours in prayer for each club, and high school expansion took place in cities[142] moving out from Dallas as seminary students became ambassadors of Rayburn's methodology.[143]

The Early Days of the Ministry

Rayburn saw Dallas as the hub of Young Life activity in those days, and perceived the base there as a transmitting station for Young Life work. Staff person Add Sewell remembered, "the night we put newsprint on the floor and got down on our hands and knees, drawing out north, south, east and west with Dallas as the hub." Staff people were assigned east to Tyler, Texas, west to Wichita Falls, Kansas and south to Houston, Texas. But Rayburn was pushed by his main supporter Herbert Taylor to expand his understanding of the scope of the ministry. Taylor prodded him: "You'll have to go national, Rayburn, or I'll not give you another dime."[144] Expansion often took place along the lines of Dallas Seminary graduates or Presbyterian ministers who had heard of Young Life work previously and wanted the ministry in their cities. Dispersal out of Dallas then went out to areas such as Bellingham, Washington and Memphis, Tennessee. After a club was established and operating smoothly, Young Life staff people[145] would often

---

142. Gainesville and the Houston area were the first outposts of Young Life work. This is what the Young Life process in the early days looked like: "On Mondays they drove to Gainesville, dropping off one at a time at Lake Dallas, Valley View, Myra, and Saint Jo. Then as club was over at the farthest point they reversed the process and collected all the club leaders on the way back" (Meredith, *It's a Sin to Bore a Kid*, 27). Rayburn would also drive a carload of leaders to Houston each week—a round trip of 480 miles.

143. Meredith, *It's a Sin to Bore a Kid*.

144. Ibid., 30.

145. After official Young Life work was started in 1941, Rayburn set about raising

move on to neighboring cities. Staff people, including Rayburn, would hang around a high school campus until someone asked what they did. "I lead Young Life clubs. Have you ever heard of Young Life? If not, I'd be happy to tell you about it." And that would open doors in the community.[146] Rayburn would often be invited to speak at school assemblies and would meet with the principal of the school and interested parents in an effort to expand Young Life ministry in whatever manner he could.

With the expansion and development of clubs in the first decade of ministry, the explosion of young people followed. Rayburn kept fairly precise details in his personal journal about the number of students attending Young Life clubs and reflected this on his first club in Gainesville: "That's how Young Life started. I didn't have in mind to start anything, but that club went from 75 to 96, and then to 100, and then to 119, and 135, and the week before finals there were 170 kids there."[147] The early tent meetings of the campaign would draw three hundred to four hundred and fifty on a nightly basis. At an all area assembly held at a Dallas hotel two thousand young people showed up to hear Rayburn speak. By 1952, Rayburn was holding his Colorado Springs club in a funeral home—the only available spot big enough to hold the crowd of 467 young people.[148]

In the annual report for 1971, Young Life provides a snapshot of statistics from 1969–1971. The number total number of full-time staff members grew from 286 to 332; they served alongside volunteers that grew in number from 2,350 to 3,699. Those staff and volunteers served a weekly average of 46,812 students in 683 clubs in 1969 to 75,233 students in 919 clubs by 1971. By 1971 the total budget for Young Life areas totaled $5,073,133.[149]

By 1974 the fiscal report as compiled by president Bill Starr noted some hesitancy in the growth of the organization. He states, "Though the figures of 1973-74 represent growth over the previous year, the fall of '74 shows almost a static situation. I do not believe this is true in the case of vital interest, and here's where I draw the distinction. I believe more young people are deeply concerned than ever before with regard to seeking an

---

funds for the four full-time staff people. After touring the US as far as Philadelphia, he had raised enough money for each staff person to earn $100 a month (Meredith, *It's a Sin to Bore a Kid*).

146. Ibid.

147. Rayburn III, *Dance, Children, Dance*, 36; Sublett, *The Diaries of Jim Rayburn*.

148. Rayburn III, *Dance, Children, Dance*. See appendix for a photograph of this club meeting.

149. Young Life, year-end report 1971, 11.

answer in the realm of the spiritual." He goes on to note that there were moderate gains in the number of staff, with an increase of sixty more full-time staff. What encouraged Starr the most for this fiscal year was the increase in volunteer staff with 350 added to the ministry. By 1974, with a budget of $7,315,443, there were 425 full-time staff people, 5196 volunteers in 1077 clubs hosting an average of 62,010 students.[150]

By the early 1990s, president Doug Burleigh had this to say about the mission of Young Life: "So, if you ask, our prognosis for Young Life in the coming years is, 'things are looking up,' because we are looking up . . . to Him."[151] In 1992, there were 55,000 high school students and 8000 junior high students were participating in five hundred clubs in North America, and 70,000 students attended a Young Life camp. There were also 16,000 students participating in Campaigners Bible study in an effort to deepen their faith in Christ. At this time, over nine hundred full-time staff and 8000 volunteer leaders operated with a budget of $45,117,000 in order to reach young people with the message of Christ. At the start of the twenty-first century, the Young Life staff (3,228 people) was ministering to 78,719 students on a weekly basis in 2,381 clubs. There were 32,550 students involved in Campaigners Bible study giving Young Life a total of 615,534 students ministered to each year. Young Life estimated they were reaching 186,000 junior high students at the same time. There were 36,819 high school and 11,970 junior high students who attended Young Life camp—all of this taking place on the Young Life budget of $180,229,476.[152]

Camping[153]

Camping within the Young Life organization also began through the vision of founder Jim Rayburn. It was his desire to see young people given a chance to step away from everyday life to a place where they could hear the good news of the Gospel in a secluded, yet spectacular, location. By 1945, four years after the organization was officially founded, Rayburn began his pursuit of purchasing property on behalf of Young Life.

---

150. Young Life, year-end report 1974, 1.
151. *Relationships*, Spring, 1992, 10.
152. These are statistics for the 2008–2009 school year; www.younglife.org.
153. The role and emphasis on camping within Young Life will be discussed in the "Cultural Expression" chapter.

After an initial deal fell through for a different camp property, Rayburn came across Star Ranch in the Colorado Mountains that he felt would be perfect for Young Life. He summoned Herbert J. Taylor and his wife from Chicago so that they could consider the possibility of Young Life purchasing the property. The cost of the property was set at $100,000 but Taylor was able to get that cut in half as he surveyed the camp. By the time Rayburn arrived in Colorado Springs, Taylor had purchased the camp on behalf of Young Life. When Taylor arrived back in Chicago he called a special board meeting to discuss the property and was shocked when the other board members did not share the enthusiasm for the camp. They didn't believe kids would be interested in traveling to Colorado for Young Life camp, and simply believed Rayburn wanted the camp property because he loved hiking and skiing. Meredith writes, "The Mitchell brothers were astounded that Taylor would share Jim's faith about this camp expense at a time when they were struggling over money to pay staff salaries. Taylor left the board meeting, sold his preferred stock in Club Aluminum, and bought Star Ranch himself."[154] Taylor leased the camp to Young Life for $1 a year for the purpose of conducting a full-scale camping program for young people.[155] Meredith believes that the start of the Colorado camping program was a key to the rapid expansion of Young Life beyond their Texas roots[156] to a national influence of young people.[157]

Within three years, capacity at Star Ranch was no longer large enough for the purpose of Young Life, so an additional camping property was sought. Just a hundred miles to the west of Star Ranch there was a camp property that caught Rayburn's attention. Nestled in the midst of the continental divide and boasting of natural hot springs on camp property, Chalk Cliff Lodge was a perfect location for the next Young Life camp. Although the buildings were run down, the staff worked diligently to give young people the best week of their lives regardless. By December of 1949, through a generous gift from the Crowell Fund, Chalk Cliff Lodge (to be renamed Silver Cliff Ranch by Young Life) became the property of the Young Life organization. Rayburn III states, "Jim's desire to have the classiest camps in the

154. Meredith, *It's a Sin to Bore a Kid*, 43.

155. Ibid; Rayburn III, *Dance, Children, Dance*; Sublett, *The Diaries of Jim Rayburn*.

156. In April of 1947, Rayburn moved the Young Life office and his family from Dallas to Star Ranch in Colorado Springs, Colorado. Now that Young Life owned property Rayburn was eager to show it off as much as possible. Young Life has its headquarters in Colorado Springs ever since. (Meredith, *It's a Sin to Bore a Kid*)

157. Ibid.

country was well on the way to being fulfilled, as both Star Ranch and Silver Cliff Ranch were prime properties in choice locations. More important was the obvious touch of God on the whole process of their acquisition."[158]

The third Young Life property was purchased within a nine-month period a year later. Round-Up Lodge, which became Frontier Ranch, was purchased with a generous donation from the owner, a doctor from St. Louis, Missouri. After dropping the purchase price to $300,000, the physician donated $50,000 to the Young Life ministry. Countering their previous reaction, the board approved the purchase of Round-Up Lodge but with the provision that Rayburn find outside donations to finance the sale. Rayburn managed to raise the money needed to purchase the camp, and only nine donors were needed to raise the $250,000.[159]

By 1954, the Young Life board was shocked to find out that Rayburn was looking at a fourth camping property for the ministry. "The Malibu Club has been built lavishly as an escape for Hollywood stars, perched on primordial rock jutting into the fiordlike [sic] waters of an inland waterway" in the Canadian west. The scenery was majestic and the camp property ready to be taken over immediately—already fully furnished from bedding to silverware. But the Malibu Club did two things to expand the vision and understanding of Young Life: first, it pushed Young Life to become an international ministry as a Canadian Trust had to be set up in order to purchase the property. Secondly, it forced Young Life to embrace what it was already living into, being a resort-style camping ministry to young people. Bill Starr states, "We'd been flirting with it ever since we got Star, then Silver Cliff, then Frontier. But we'd never really defined it. When we got Malibu, we had to face completely the fact that we were operating on a *resort* concept—which at that time was a very new and daring way to go in the Christian community."[160] The first summer of camping at Malibu saw seven hundred campers as well as a number of drop-in guests[161] who came upon the camp while yachting in the bay.[162]

---

158. Rayburn III, *Dance, Children, Dance*, 78.

159. Meredith, *It's a Sin to Bore a Kid*; Sublett, *The Diaries of Jim Rayburn*.

160. Meredith, *It's a Sin to Bore a Kid*, 66.

161. The first summer at Malibu saw a visit from the United States senator Henry Jackson and his wife along with their guests: John and Jacqueline Kennedy (Sublett, *The Diaries of Jim Rayburn*).

162. Sublett, *The Diaries of Jim Rayburn*.

From these early roots of Young Life and the evolution through camping they have expanded their camping ministry to all corners of the world. They currently maintain twenty camps across North and Central America and also lease camps for their use across the globe. Young Life states:

> Young Life camping involves high adventure, lots of fun, great food and excellent speakers who understand and respect high school and middle school kids. At Young Life's 20 camps in North and Central America, kids are treated to resort-quality facilities for which Young Life has become known. But Young Life camping happens all over the world; in some cases we own or lease camps and in other locations we get creative. Regardless of the facility, the experience is the same—kids getting away from the pressures of everyday life, having fun with friends and their Young Life leaders, and hearing the message of God's love in terms they can understand. And Young Life camping is open to kids who often are overlooked: those from economically depressed communities, kids with disabilities and teenage mothers. Each year, almost 90,000 kids around the world spend a week or a weekend at Young Life camp, having an experience that many describe as the best of their lives.[163]

Presidents

The previous sections highlighted staff, club and camping statistics that have been documented by the Young Life ministry. From the original notations of club ministry numbers in the journal of founder Jim Rayburn,[164] to current ministry statistics in the *Relationships* magazine, Young Life has always been cognizant of the number of young people they were reaching with the news of Jesus Christ. In this section I focus on the work of current president Denny Rydberg for two reasons: Because he is the current president of the Young Life organization and the emphasis of his ministry highlights the focus of the ministry today, and because of his heavy emphasis on numbers and statistics within the ministry. I believe the emphasis Rydberg places on numbers and statistics deviates from the incarnational and relational emphasis of past presidents.[165]

163. Young Life Camping, www.younglife.org/camping.
164. Sublett, *The Diaries of Jim Rayburn*.
165. Past presidents, other than founder Jim Rayburn, include: Bill Starr, Bob Mitchell, Doug Burleigh, and Ted Johnson who served as interim president before the hiring of Denny Rydberg.

History

Denny Rydberg was hired as president of Young Life in 1993 becoming the first person outside of the Young Life ministry to take up the position of president. Rydberg immediately set forth to grow the ministry of Young Life through an aggressive training program that sought to increase the number of leaders, clubs, and young people involved in the organization. Rydberg continually set forth his goal for the organization and touts what Young Life was trying to accomplish. Constantly putting forth the percentages and numbers, Rydberg sets a tone for the ministry based on statistics. Using scripture in conjunction with the vision for the organization, Rydberg reminds readers in *Relationships* magazine of where Young Life is going in the Fall/Winter editorial of 1998. "The Great Race" editorial on Hebrews 12:1-3:

> In Young Life, we're involved in a version of that race. Our part of the race involves an attempt to increase our outreach to kids 400 percent in 10 years. That seems as laughable as someone asking me to do the Ironman with no preparation. Absolutely impossible! But God reaching 400 percent more kids through Young Life is not. And it's not impossible if we follow the teaching of the author of Hebrews. What are we to do? One, remember the crowd. We are surrounded by a great cloud of witnesses who cheer us on.... Two, cast off everything that hinders and the sin that so easily entangles. ... Three, run with perseverance. Remember the marathoner's prayer: "If you can lift it up, Lord, I can put it down." Four, fix our eyes on Jesus...[166]

In order to reach these high expectations and numbers within Young Life, leaders of the organization came up with a system of training they termed RTD—recruiting, training and deploying. In an article titled "One Giant Leap" in the Fall/Winter 1998 issue they explain:

> While most of the world is counting down to the year 2000, Young Life staffers are counting down instead to the year 2006—and for good reason. In 1996, an aggressive goal was born in the minds of senior leadership—a goal to increase the number of schools with Young Life to 7,000 in just 10 years—an increase of more than 400 percent! Yes, it was a solar-system-sized goal, but with a foundation of prayer and a navigation system called RTD—Recruiting, Training, Deploying—the plan was launched and the mission was underway. In the spirit of John F. Kennedy's grand plan to put a man on the moon, Young Life President Denny Rydberg and his

---

166. *Relationships,* Fall/Winter 1998, 3.

senior leadership team created this shoot-for-the-moon, 7,000-by-2006 goal. Both goals were set knowing that significant structures for that kind of progress did not yet exist. "Ours was a bold goal, but carried out in stages and with lots of prayer, it was always an obtainable goal," says Mike O'Leary, vice president of RTD.[167]

The first stage in the development of RTD began when Rydberg called together forty leaders in the spring of 1994 to create a plan. The called this first stage the "Friendship Stage," and planned on recruiting 2,500 full and part-time field staff to begin the recruiting and training stages of the program. This would increase the number of staff by three times the number employed in 1995. At this point of planning, Young Life had not registered growth in the organization for a decade. Mike O'Leary, vice president of RTD, stated Young Life had a reputation for great vision but "spotty training." The next stage of training was coined the "Gemini Stage." One hundred and thirteen people attended New Staff Training in 1995 thus began the internship phase of the RTD program. This new internship program is a two-year intensive program that requires interns to receive seminary instruction as well as local ministry apprenticeship. Young Life saw results of this internship program (as well as a newly developed Area Director School) quickly: "After three full years of implementation, God's blessing is evident. In 1998, Young Life recruited 230 new full-time staff. And coupled with the explosive growth of part-time staff people, the mission has seen a 9 percent increase in the number of clubs—finishing out last year with 158 new clubs across the U.S."[168]

In the early stages of this new training program, Young Life could not imagine their successful early trend might stop in the future. "It's humbling to see such an aggressive goal actually steamroll ahead so successfully," says Denny Rydberg. "We can't let up, but with God's help, I don't see any letting up in sight. I'm just so grateful to all the Young Life staff who have worked so hard to make this bold venture an ongoing success."[169] With enthusiasm for the training program at a high level, and the ten-year goal being so many years away, Young Life could not fathom a lack of success in meeting their goal of 400 percent growth in the organization. Concluding this article, the authors used one final metaphor from the US space program. "... to steal a Neil Armstrong line in regard to our RTD program. In 2006,

167. Ibid.
168. Ibid., 15.
169. Ibid., 16.

we'll look back and say . . . This was one small step for God, one giant leap for Young Life"[170]

The following year, in an editorial titled "When Facing the Impossible," Rydberg uses the story of the feeding of the 5,000 to frame his understanding for growth within Young Life. Those involved with Young Life, those involved with reaching the goal of growth within the organization, could easily place themselves in the position of trying to feed so many people with so little resources. Rydberg could imagine Young Life staff and volunteers could feel like the disciples—"frustrated, baffled and stumped." He imagines that they could feel his request was impossible. Restating the goal, Rydberg confesses Young Life has embarked on an impossible mission—aiming to be in 7,000 schools by the year 2006. He goes on to say, "We're in approximately 2,500 and we have 4,500 to go in the next seven years. But the 'Feeding of the 7,000' has already begun. Jesus has already taken our limited resources and is multiplying them as we see more staff, volunteers and money bouncing in our baskets. When He tells us to feed the hungry, we need to do what we're doing now. Take the resources we have, give them to Jesus and watch Him do the impossible!"[171] With God on the side of Young Life, the ten-year goal was not impossible, but seen as possible through the work of Jesus and the Holy Spirit.

By 2002, Rydberg has come to recognize the work and goals of Young Life cannot be accomplished by staff alone. In a Summer 2002 editorial titled, "Have I Got an Opportunity for You," Rydberg lays out some understanding of what it means to volunteer to be a team leader within a Young Life club. Rydberg explains that as a leader of a team, you will take responsibility for leading outreach to a school campus and that "You are responsible for a whole bunch of kids meeting Jesus Christ and growing in their faith. Are you having fun yet?"[172] Rydberg states that his request is simple but the execution of the request is very difficult. The leader of a Young Life team is responsible for recruiting other volunteers to help lead club and to receive training from the area director, regional director and other training initiatives. The leader will be responsible for impacting a school in the best way and meeting kids. The team will need to decide how to lead club in the most effective way and how to recruit kids to go to camp, raising money so none

---

170. *Relationships*, Fall/Winter 1998, 5–16. Further discussion on the imprint of American metaphor is found in chapter four, "Cultural Expression."

171. *Relationships*, Spring/Summer, 1999, 3.

172. *Relationships*, Summer, 2002, 2.

are left behind. Rydberg also believes that when leaders take responsibility for a specific school they will pray like never before and their heart will soar and break as they walk with kids from that community. He finishes by stating, "We've grown at an astonishing rate. More kids have met Christ and are growing in their faith. But we'll never get to 7,500 on the backs of paid staff. We have to be a volunteer organization at every level to succeed. In addition to volunteers on the local committee and volunteers involved in direct ministry to kids, we need volunteers to lead the ministry at a school . . ."[173] Finally, Rydberg asks questions and lays out priorities for those thinking about becoming a leader of a Young Life club: "Do you love Christ? Do you love kids? Would you like to see your life count by helping kids meet Christ? Are you teachable and trainable? Do you sense God speaking to you? If you are able to answer all of these questions positively, you hold the skills Young Life is looking for."[174]

With the vision established (400% growth for the ministry), the system in which to achieve that growth (RTD), the *Young Life* magazine of the new millennium started to include within its pages a "Ministry Update" that gave a snapshot of the numbers Young Life wanted to highlight in certain areas. Most often these ministry updates included numbers in conjunction with the amount of growth within the ministry, but it also highlighted Rydberg's expanding vision for Latino and international ministry within Young Life. The editorial page within *Relationships* magazine became the template for inspiring growth within the mission, recruiting adults to be leaders for the mission, and focusing the staff on the direction of the ministry. As the ten-year goal progressed, Rydberg began looking for ways to continually showcase the growth of Young Life.

In the Fall 2004 issue of *Relationships* magazine, Rydberg begins with a celebration of the All Staff Conference that met in Orlando, Florida. As the conference gave energy and resources to staff for the coming years, Rydberg focused on the improvement in numbers for the ministry:

> We turned the world upside down this year as we looked for lost kids through 3,726 ministries in the United States and 438 ministries in 47 countries across the sea. We turned a couple of camps upside down as well as we hosted the first-ever camp specifically for kids with disabilities at Crooked Creek Ranch and our second-ever camp for teen moms at Lost Canyon. We continued to spend

173. Ibid.
174. Ibid., 2.

our last ounce of energy and all the resources at our disposal searching for lost kids here at home, in the cities, in the suburbs, in rural areas and small towns.... Every kid, everywhere, for eternity. Thank you for joining us in this relentless search.[175]

Continuing his appreciation for statistics, Rydberg emphasizes specific numbers attributed to international ministry[176] within the Young Life organization. In the editorial titled "Kids around the World: Young Life's Global Commitment" Rydberg states: "95 percent of kids live *outside* the United States and 95 percent of youth workers work *within* the United States.... Now we're in 54 countries from A to T (Armenia to Tanzania). We have 453 total ministries with 126 U.S. staff, 178 international staff and 2484 volunteer leaders. That's progress and a good start but it's barely scratching the surface of what we want to accomplish. We want to renew our focus on international. We want to build sustainable movements more than we do individual ministries."[177] Rydberg was challenging those within the organization to strategize about the best possible way to reach those 95 percent of young people who live outside of the United States. He acknowledges that within any mission movement two things are needed: people and money. Rydberg finishes by stating, "*Please pray*—that the Lord will raise up workers for the harvest field. *Please consider*—that the Lord may be calling you to join the team and go. *Please give*—generously and hilariously to our efforts worldwide. We are an international outreach to kids everywhere. And, with the Lord's guidance and generosity, we will impact more kids wherever they happen to live in the years to come."[178] Prayer—praying that God will raise up workers. People—acknowledge that you might be one of those people being called to serve in international ministry. Money—give "generously and hilariously" to the work of Young Life.

175. *Relationships*, Fall 2004, 11.

176. Rydberg also emphasized this international work in the Fall 2006 issue of the YLM in his editorial titled "Northern Exposure." He states, "Young Life is a growing, international ministry. What is happening in the Former Soviet Union, Scandinavia and through our military ministry is happening in more than 50 countries. The International divisions are the fastest growing divisions in Young Life. More nationals are coming on staff. Camps opened this year in Tanzania for the first time. In Ethiopia, national staff led all their camps. We have a presence in Asia, Latin America, the Caribbean, the United Kingdom, Europe and Africa. God is moving and we have the privilege of being part of it" (*Relationships,* Fall, 2006, 2).

177. *Relationships*, Winter, 2006, 2.

178. Ibid., 2.

Here I have shown the numbers focused leadership of current Young Life president Denny Rydberg. Within three years of his presidency, Rydberg established an aggressive campaign for growth within the Young Life organization. Because of this, a new recruiting and training program (RTD) was established in order to provide leaders for the new areas and schools where Young Life was in operation. After surprising initial success in the ten-year goal, Rydberg began to focus attention on the growth of international ministry. By 2006, the end of the ten-year goal, there was little attention or fanfare for the conclusion of Rydberg's plan.[179] Today the Young Life ministry has grown to over 3,000 full-time staff working in 4,500 locations in 58 countries around the world. Sixteen thousand volunteers and 11,000 committee members joined staff to minister to over 1 million young people. Young Life's twenty properties serve over 90,000 young people each year.[180]

Conclusion

The Young Life organization is often associated with other evangelical parachurch ministries from the 1940s because of the parallel establishment of the Miracle Book Club, Youth for Christ, and InterVarsity Christian Fellowship. However, Young Life made a distinct mark within evangelical youth ministries by emphasizing adventure and a relaxed, relational style of ministry through incarnational presence. As noted above, Rayburn improvised in youth ministry until stumbling upon a high school club and camping methodology that would work well with young people. Rayburn, and the staff and leadership that followed, established Young Life as a model to be copied by other ministries over the years. Though often at odds with the institutional church and straining towards a New Testament understanding of Christianity, Rayburn and Young Life were influential in laying a foundation for incarnational ministry that has been utilized within youth ministries today. In the following chapter I will review the doctrinal statements and understanding of the Young Life organization showing how Young Life articulates the doctrinal position of their ministry in a distinct way.

---

179. A new goal has recently been established by Rydberg called "Reaching a World of Kids" (RWOK) that has been quietly inserted within the ministry (July 2009 field notes).

180. Sublett, *The Diaries of Jim Rayburn*; www.younglife.org.

2

Formal Doctrine

I STILL HAVE THE hand drawn sketch tucked away in the back of my Bible. I was in my second year of high school and working through my questions of how this relationship with Jesus really worked. As I was asking my Young Life leader one question after another she finally got out a piece of paper and sketched the bridge diagram.

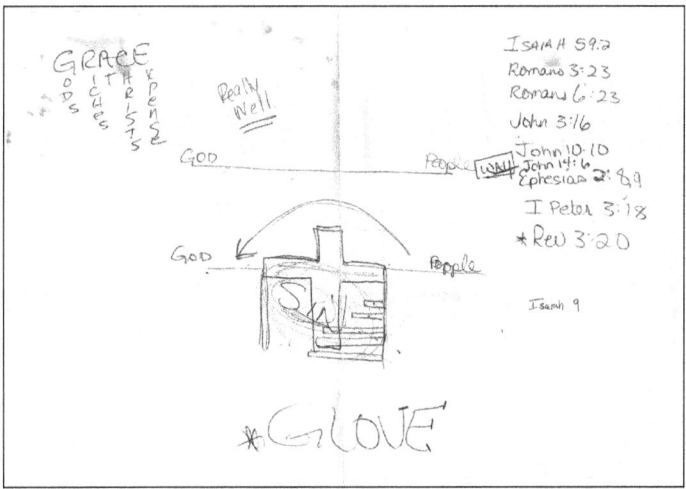

It is a simple explanation of God on one side, an empty expanse in the middle, and humanity on the other. We are meant to be in relationship with God but our sin is the empty expanse we cannot cross in order to be in God's presence. The cross of Christ, however, fills that expanse and allows us a bridge to cross in order to return to God once again. The diagram, in it's simplicity yet complexity, was extremely helpful in allowing my teenage brain a way to grasp the wonders of a relationship with God. However, as I stated earlier, as I came towards the end of my career with Young Life I got stuck in the simplicity of usual Young Life stories and explanations and was left with the question of "is this it?"

Jeff McSwain, a former area director in North Carolina, describes what he understands by Young Life's praxis theology of evangelism. Citing the foundation of the Young Life club where adult leaders make every young person feel welcome, McSwain believes young people appreciate belonging in a place that is safe and nonjudgmental. This reflects the life of Christ. But McSwain goes on to state, "However, as great as this sense of *practical belonging* is, one of the issues that Young Life has wrestled with since its inception is the question of how much *theological belonging* to give unreached teenagers."[1] Though Young Life might be well versed in providing space for practical belonging of young people, McSwain believes the theological space for young people is lacking. And I believe this comes from the standpoint of Young Life resisting the intellectual component of theology. In a training manual from 1969 they state, "And with all of this we must continually resist the temptation to intellectualize Christianity. We dare not give the impression that to know the right answers is all that God requires. Our intellectual grasp of theology may be a help or a great hindrance to us as teachers. We dare not become 'stuffed shirts.'"[2]

From the foundation of the conservative, evangelical church, the emerging youth consumer culture, as well as post-WWII revivalism, Young Life began its innovative practice of ministry. Although Young Life was formed in parallel manner to other conservative, evangelical youth ministries of the 1940s, Young Life gives distinct voice to theological terms that shape the Christian church. The purpose of this chapter is to expand the understanding of the ministry of Young Life as they articulate the doctrinal stance they take as an organization and the distinct voice they give to theological terms such as Christology, soteriology, discipleship and ecclesiology. Young Life establishes its ministerial practice on the foundation of incarnational theology, and I argue that their doctrinal understanding flows from this foundation. However, I begin with a review of the doctrinal statements of Youth for Christ and InterVarsity Christian Fellowship in order to show what forms their respective theological stance and the time

---

1. McSwain, "Young Life and the Gospel of All-Along Belonging."
2. Young Life, training manual, 10.

at which they documented those beliefs. I then review the formal doctrinal statements of Young Life that are found in the Statement of Faith document as well as the Non-Negotiable Gospel Proclamation document to provide an in-depth review of what shapes Young Life. Though Youth for Christ and InterVarsity Christian Fellowship were formed at a similar time as Young Life, they articulated their formal statements of faith at an earlier stage than did Young Life. This, I argue, is an example of the methodological rather than theological emphasis of Young Life. Young Life was content to follow the path of practical innovation in youth ministry rather than theological definitiveness. Using a variety of sources from archival material gathered from the Young Life headquarters I was able to formulate a perspective of the Christian message they share via a variety of communication devices. From magazines to business cards to training materials Young Life presents their doctrinal understanding from not only formal statements of faith, but through the material they present to young people and adults alike. I begin, then, with the doctrinal statements of Youth for Christ and InterVarsity Christian Fellowship in order to demonstrate that Young Life articulates a different understanding of Christian doctrine that focused more heavily on praxis rather than statements of faith.

Statements of Faith for Youth for Christ and InterVarsity Christian Fellowship

In the previous chapter I explored how evangelical youth ministries of the 1940s were influenced by trends in the United States at the time of their foundation. From the emergence of the evangelical church to the growing youth culture to post-WWII revivalism, numerous variants provided shaping influence over youth ministries at that time. However, youth ministries like Youth for Christ and InterVarsity Christian Fellowship worked to clearly articulate the Christian doctrine that provided the ultimate foundations for their ministries. This section will briefly discuss the Christian doctrine that was emphasized by each group, highlighting the statements of faith that provided formal structure for the organizations.

Youth for Christ was officially organized at the Winona Lake Bible Conference in 1945.[3] Pahl notes that Youth for Christ articulated their doctrinal position in conjunction with the National Association of Evangelicals

3. Pahl, *Youth Ministry in Modern America*; Senter, *The Coming Revolution in Youth Ministry*; Carpenter, *Revive Us Again*.

that was organized at approximately the same time. Youth for Christ published their statement of faith in every issue of their magazine, reminding readers of their basic beliefs. Beliefs included: the infallibility of the Bible; the trinity; the deity and miracles of Jesus; salvation through regeneration; living a godly life; resurrection of both the saved and the lost; and the spiritual unity amongst believers.[4] Youth for Christ also established four key elements that formed the basis of their constitution. The constitution, sketched in the first meeting at Winona Lake in 1945, set about the work of joining separate evangelical efforts to reach young people into one unified body. The four main emphases of Youth for Christ in the original constitution set out to:

1. Promote and help win youth for Christ everywhere
2. Encourage evangelism everywhere
3. Emphasize radiant, victorious Christian living
4. Foster international service of youth through existing agencies.[5]

InterVarsity Christian Fellowship articulated their statement of faith around the same time as Youth for Christ. In the United States, InterVarsity began as an export of ministry to university students from Great Britain. As InterVarsity chapters grew in number and strength—in 1947 one hundred and fifty new chapters were formed—the leadership of C. Stacey Woods and Charles Troutman concluded that a set of basic beliefs of InterVarsity should be laid out for theological consistency that would distinguish the

---

4. Pahl, *Youth Ministry in Modern America*. This is in line with what both Collins and Hunter consider broad themes found within evangelicalism. The themes, according to Collins, include: (1) The normative value of Scripture in the Christian life, (2) The necessity of conversion (whether or not dramatic or even remembered), (3) The cruciality of the atoning work of Christ as the sole mediator between God and humanity, and (4) The imperative of evangelism, of proclaiming the glad tidings of salvation to a lost and hurting world (Collins, *The Evangelical Movement*, 21). To a greater or lesser extent, Marsden, Hunter and Bebbgington include similar traits of evangelical emphases in their list of broad evangelical characteristics. Hunter states that, behaviorally, evangelicals are individuated and orientated towards an experiential faith with a conviction for proselytizing nonbelievers. Their orientation towards spiritual salvation and religiosity can be characterized by the doctrinal understanding of: (1) The belief that the Bible is the inerrant Word of God, (2) The belief in the divinity of Christ, and (3) The belief in the efficacy of Christ's life, death, and physical resurrection for the salvation of the human soul (Hunter, *American Evangelicalism*, 7).

5. Larson, *Youth for Christ*, 88; Cannister, *Starting Right*, 88.

work in the United States from that of Great Britain and Canada. Hunt states,

> The Basis of Faith was thoughtfully and carefully hammered out in this climate of theological tension. It was basic, not comprehensive, but easy to understand. It was simple; it was bedrock; it was fundamentalist. (The word *evangelical* was not commonly used in the 1940s.) It reflected a biblical response to contemporary issues:
>
> 1. The unique, divine inspiration, integrity and authority of the Bible.
> 2. The deity of our Lord Jesus Christ.
> 3. The necessity and efficacy of the substitutionary death of Jesus Christ for the redemption of the world, and the historic fact of his bodily resurrection.
> 4. The presence and power of the Holy Spirit in the work of regeneration.
> 5. The consummation of the kingdom in the "glorious appearing of the great God and our Savior Jesus Christ."[6]

Like Youth for Christ and the evangelical predecessors before them, InterVarsity followed suit in laying out evangelical guidelines that would earmark their work and give formation to their outreach on the campuses of colleges and universities in the United States. Like other evangelical institutions, InterVarsity believed in the authority of Christ and the Bible, the redemption of Christ through his death on the cross, and the importance of the Holy Spirit. But indirectly they emphasized personal quiet time, corporate Bible study, and the outreach to and evangelism of peers. Hunt believes that "The InterVarsity movement came as a new kind of Christianity, a deeper, a more life-encompassing relationship with God through Christ than we had ever known before."[7]

By the mid 1940s, both Youth for Christ and InterVarsity had outlined their official statements of faith, as well as come to some understanding of the emphases of their ministries. Both articulate the deity of Jesus Christ, the power of the Holy Spirit, and the resurrection of the body. Also, both informally emphasized the importance of evangelism as an outgrowth of a changed life. However, as I will emphasize in this chapter, the Young Life

6. Hunt and Hunt, *For Christ and the University*, 81.
7. Ibid., 85.

organization did not formulate their statements of faith as Youth for Christ and InterVarsity did, but focused their energies on perfecting their praxis of belief. This is an important difference to distinguish because, while Youth for Christ or InterVarsity may be able to articulate their understanding of Christianity, Young Life placed their emphasis on the action of ministry. This chapter, however, will articulate both the practical and theological belonging as put forth by the Young Life organization.

I have briefly reviewed the formal statements of faith and the operational guidelines that gave shape to both Youth for Christ and InterVarsity Christian Fellowship. It is important to note that both organizations established these statements of faith in the early stages of their ministry—both setting out to specify the trajectory of their work and to clarify their theological positions. However, as I will set out in the following section, Young Life did not articulate a specific theological stance until much later in the life of the organization. I will now review in depth the words of both their Statement of Faith (1974) as well as their Non-Negotiable Gospel Proclamation (2007) document in order to delineate their official theological position.

Formal Doctrinal Statements: The Young Life Statement of Faith and Non-Negotiable Gospel Proclamation

In the previous section I set forth the statements of faith for both the Youth for Christ and InterVarsity Christian Fellowship ministries, highlighting both the content as well as the year formalized for each group. Youth for Christ, in solidifying their statement of faith in 1945, and InterVarsity ratifying their statement of faith in 1947, preceded Young Life in formal statements of faith by at least twenty-five years. Though Young Life lagged behind other evangelical youth ministries in articulating their beliefs formally, they nonetheless documented those tenets that give structure to their ministry. In this section the official statements of belief as presented by Young Life are reviewed in order to gain an understanding of their official theological position and how they intend to put those beliefs into action. As stated in the introduction to this thesis, Young Life has gone through a season of theological debate within the ministry. Because of this theological debate, it became apparent to me that the two documents of the Statement of Faith as well as the Non-Negotiable document need to be held in conjunction with one another in order to have a full understanding of their theological position.

However, through my research I discovered Young Life articulated their official position on faith at a much later date than other evangelical youth ministries.[8] As I showed in the previous chapter, Young Life positioned themselves in a doctrinally innovative way through their understanding of incarnational theology. I also showed how incarnational theology has framed their articulation of theological terms such as Christology, soteriology, discipleship and ecclesiology in a relational manner. Could the Young Life organization been influenced by the strict, conservative upbringing of Jim Rayburn that paid more attention to the rules of faith rather than the joy of life in Christ? Or was Young Life resistant to state their theological tenets because of the tense relationship with denominational churches? Perhaps it was the loss of Young Life staff people to seminary training that made them resistant to theological positioning? It is speculation for the reason of a late articulation of theological belief.

The "Non-Negotiables of Young Life's Gospel Proclamation" (2007) is a relatively recent document, meant to bring clarification to the staff and volunteers of the organization in the arena of Gospel proclamation. They have established this document on three tenets: The Statement of Faith, what Jim Rayburn believed and stated, and what has been historically understood as the mode of operation within the ministry. Theological disagreements[9] have taken place over the confession of Christ as Savior as the token of salvation, and there have been opinions taken on both sides of the argument. As Young Life went through the process of producing this document[10] they clarified their official position on theological issues within the ministry. However, as I will demonstrate in the following sections, Young Life began to informally structure their Christian understanding by their praxis of ministry. I argue that through their methodology of practice,

---

8. Although it is difficult to state a specific date when the first Young Life statement of faith was produced, I did uncover this statement in the archives that is helpful in garnering an idea of a basic time frame for the first completion of this document: "Three important Task Forces have been in operation throughout the year. One concerns the Statement of Faith—the final form of which is now ready. The Management Team has reviewed very carefully the basic purpose of Young Life and has come up with a paper concerning affirmations of our purpose" (Young Life, year-end report 1974, 2).

9. These disagreements will be discussed later in the chapter.

10. Even though it was originally intended as an internal document it is now in the public sphere through various avenues.

Young Life was structuring their beliefs decades earlier than their formal theological statements of faith.

Fuller Seminary theologian Ray Anderson, once remarked, "I have long thought that Young Life discovered a praxis theology of evangelism without really working through the basic foundations for it." Jeff McSwain, in reflecting on the words of Anderson, believed that Young Life should begin with a biblical rather than natural or existential basis. Both Anderson and McSwain were challenging Young Life not to simply insert biblical truths to their praxis, but to establish a foundation of theological understanding that would guide the mission in the future.[11]

The Young Life Statement of Faith

The Young Life Statement of Faith begins with a preamble and proceeds to cover eight articles of faith in the document.[12] In the preamble it is stated the central purpose of the Young Life mission is to proclaim the gospel of Jesus Christ and introduce young people to Christ in an effort to help them grow in their faith. The Statement of Faith sets out all those who affirm the document–trustees, staff, volunteers, and those who instruct at Young Life schools. The statement then proceeds to outline their eight articles of faith.

The first article affirms that scripture, of the Old and New Testament as given by divine inspiration from God, is the final authority on matters of faith and conduct. Article II proceeds to expand on their understanding of what scripture has to say—that God is a living and true God and the creator of all things. God is understood to exist in Trinitarian form: Father, Son and Holy Spirit, and that God is loving and righteous. The creative God is touched upon in Article III, describing the creative work of God as an intention to live with us in fellowship. Because of this intention, God created man and woman in his image. But, because we are sinful and incapable of a right relationship with God we are estranged from God by our disobedience. It is only by divine grace that we are capable of a right relationship with God. Article IV then describes how a right relationship is established,

---

11. McSwain, "Young Life and the Gospel of All-Along Belonging."

12. A copy of this document may be found on the Young Life website: www.younglife.org/AboutYoungLife/StatementOfFaith. The statement was first drafted during the presidency of Bill Starr (McSwain, "Young Life and the Gospel of All-Along Belonging") but it is unknown how many versions there have been of the statement since its original writing. According to the Young Life website, the last revision was made in 2007.

Formal Doctrine

through the mediating work Jesus Christ, described as God's eternal Son who was fully man and fulfilled our humanity by his life of perfect obedience. Article V explains how the mediating work of Christ was fulfilled by his death in our place, removing our guilt and reconciling us to God. Through this sacrifice Christ revealed divine love and divine justice. This article also affirms Christ's bodily resurrection from death and his ascension into heaven—there Christ rules over all things and intercedes on our behalf. Article VI speaks to the work of the Holy Spirit. It is "through the proclamation of the Gospel" that we are renewed and persuaded to confess Christ as Lord. It is also by the Holy Spirit that we are led trust in divine mercy, we are justified by faith, adopted into God's family, and enabled to live in the world so that people may see good works and grace at work in our lives. The statement of faith proceeds then to their understanding of church in Article VII: By God and his word and Spirit, we are called into fellowship with Christ's body that is the church. Young Life describes this as "one holy, catholic and apostolic church, united in love and given gifts by the Holy Spirit." The article goes on to state that the Spirit also summons us to preach the Gospel and administer sacraments, be a ministry of reconciliation, and finally, to strive for social justice. Article VIII then concludes by stating the redemptive work of God will be completed with the return of Christ when he will raise the dead, judge all people and establish his kingdom. At the time of Christ's return, those who are apart from God will be separated eternally, but those who believe shall reign with God forever.[13]

I have reviewed the preamble and eight articles of faith as presented by the Young Life organization and affirmed as the guide to their proclamation of the Gospel of Christ. The Statement of Faith is a concise affirmation of the beliefs of the organization, ranging from the biblical foundation to the person and redemptive quality of Jesus Christ. Covering the role of Christians as followers of Christ, the Statement of Faith calls for the administering of sacraments and the work of social justice. Christ will return for final judgment and those who believe will reign with Christ forever. However, as stated in the introduction to this thesis, Young Life has gone through a period of theological discernment and through this process has produced a second document that outlines the articles of faith that provides structure to their ministry. I will now review the Non-Negotiable document of Young Life illustrating the nuances in comparison to the Statement of Faith.

---

13. Young Life, "Statement."

The Non-Negotiable Gospel Proclamation Document

As I have just reviewed, the Young Life Statement of Faith outlines eight fundamental beliefs that guide the work of the Young Life ministry. However, the articles as presented in the Statement of Faith are basic in nature, making simple statements of belief without expansion or explanation. The Non-Negotiable Proclamation then becomes an important document to hold in conjunction with the Statement of Faith because it takes the articles of faith as presented in the Statement of Faith and expands upon their meaning or understanding of how they should be utilized within the organization. As noted previously, the Non-Negotiable document of Young Life was produced in 2007 in order to clarify theological discrepancies and disagreements amongst the staff and within the organization. The Non-Negotiable document consists of six "essentials" that Young Life affirms through their gospel proclamation and expands upon the six points as the document proceeds.

The "Non-Negotiables of Young Life's Gospel Proclamation"[14] is an eight-page document that was first released in October 2007.[15] From the beginning of the document, the purpose of Young Life ministry is stated clearly: "We exist to introduce adolescents to Jesus Christ and help them grow in their faith."[16] Because of the breadth of the organization[17] and the diversity in background of both staff and volunteers, the authors felt a clear presentation of the gospel should be communicated. They want to be explicit in their presentation, true to Scripture, the mission's history, as well as the Young Life Statement of Faith.[18] This document, produced for

---

14. The language of "non-negotiable" is not a new phrase for Young Life. You can find this phrase used in relation to non-negotiables of Young Life camp as found in their leadership-training manual (1994).

15. Young Life released a revised version of this document in November, 2007. I am using the original document in order to capture the language that Young Life first used in relationship to their non-negotiable proclamation.

16. Jim Rayburn was asked to state what Young Life was in the August 1954 issue of the *Young Life* magazine. He said, "Young Life is a group of people who are trying to find out how to get young people to listen to the most wonderful message in the world" (*Young Life* magazine, August 1954, 4).

17. Young Life operates in fifty-two countries around the world as well as in all fifty states in the U.S. Three thousand staff people and thirty thousand volunteers serve nearly one million young people annually (www.younglife.org).

18. Young Life, "Non-Negotiables," 1.

staff use,[19] states the intent for the document in this way: "The intent of the paper is not to squelch the creativity of the staff, but to provide a foundation on which their creativity can be expressed. However, these are not suggestions. They are key elements of what we will present and what our audiences can expect when they are involved with Young Life."[20] Again, quoting Jim Rayburn, Young Life acknowledges it has always been a Christ-centered mission. "Jesus is not just what Young Life is all about. Jesus is all that Young Life is about."[21]

The Non-Negotiable document outlines six key points for the communication of the Young Life message.[22] First, they desire to proclaim the person of Jesus Christ in every message. Second, they proclaim the reality of sin and the consequence of it—that we are incapable of a right relationship with God apart from the grace of God. Third, they proclaim that the crucifixion of Jesus is the solution to this problem of sin, and the ultimate proof of God's love. Fourth, they proclaim the resurrection of Jesus Christ. Fifth, they invite high school, middle school, and college age friends to confess Jesus as Lord in response to the risen Christ's offer of salvation. And finally, they proclaim a call to discipleship by encouraging those who respond to grow in their faith.[23] The structure of the Non-Negotiable document is such that they make their proclamations in each point, and support those proclamations with various articles of faith from the Statement of Faith. This indicates that they are placing an emphasis on the Non-Negotiable document and using the Statement of Faith as a secondary but supportive resource of authority.

1) We proclaim the Person of Jesus Christ in every message.

Under the first proclamation, Young Life asserts that sharing Gospel narratives with young people is what makes the organization distinctive. Their intention is to help young people see Christ as an amazing person who cares for them, and they believe most young people do not have a clear understanding of his character, personality, or power. They therefore state

19. They declare this intention in their disclaimer to the document (www.younglife.org).
20. Young Life, "Non-Negotiables," 1.
21. Ibid., 2.
22. I list them here and a deeper explanation will follow later in the chapter.
23. Young Life, "Non-Negotiables," 1.

that, "Our message is Jesus."[24] Noting the belief that salvation history is both originated and culminated in Christ and God's redemptive purposes are found in Christ, they proclaim that every talk will center on a Gospel account of Jesus.[25] Young Life utilizes Article II (the Trinitarian nature of God) and Article IV (Christ is the mediator between God and humanity) as affirmation of this proclamation, noting that the organization is and has always been a Christ-centered mission. The first proclamation concludes with a quote from Jim Rayburn, "First, we must stick to presenting Jesus Christ. There are all kinds of secondary things we could get involved in, but they aren't Young Life's business. We are not to 'major in minors,' but in the one all-important essential: that Jesus Christ is our greatest need, and that He's all we need."[26]

2) We proclaim the reality of sin and its consequences—that apart from divine grace, we are estranged from God by our disobedience and incapable of a right relationship with God.

Under the second proclamation, Young Life outlines sin and its consequences as a relational issue—sin is a consequence of a broken relationship with God so, "relational words such as *estrangement, alienation, lostness* and *purposelessness*" represent humanity's condition. They also use words such as "*guilty, rebellious, separated* and *condemned*" as descriptions that would characterize sinful humanity.[27] Young Life believes that Scripture does teach that sin is a present reality that makes humanity unable to live an abundant, eternal life apart from God.[28] They state that in the proclamation about sin, it should be presented that the reality of sin is what defines our condition and behavior—the truth of this sinfulness is both individually and corporately understood. However, Young Life also insists that Jesus should

24. Ibid., 2.

25. Within the first proclamation they do reference possible exceptions to proclaiming Christ in every message noting that a first night message at summer camp could focus on God as creator, or a second semester talk in club when an epistle is used as the Scripture passage (Ibid., 2).

26. Ibid., 2.

27. Ibid., 3.

28. They use these Scripture passages as evidence of the sinful nature of humanity and inability to live abundant, eternal life apart from God: Gal 3:22; John 8:24; 1 John 5:11–12; Rom 3:10–18.

be present in any presentation about sin, there should be no distinction between God and Jesus. As affirmed in their understanding of a Trinitarian God, love and justice are present in all three persons—God, Jesus, and the Holy Spirit. Young people should not be given the impression that God is content to condemn sinful humanity while Jesus is presented as the caring and forgiving one. Young Life also notes within the second proclamation that a moralistic communication of the Gospel is not sufficient in creating a right relationship with God. Ceasing to do bad things does not bring salvation; humanity is accountable before God both for rebellion and for sinful actions. The second proclamation concludes with counsel on the method of presenting the reality of sin to young people. Young Life stresses it is not the effectiveness of the presentation that will convict young people about their sinfulness, but it will be through the movement of the Holy Spirit. They go on to note that young people should not be left to wallow in their sin or forcing them to go hours before they hear the hope of the Good News, but should be allowed to respond to God's love and justice simultaneously. The Young Life organization affirms this proclamation using the latter half of Article IV from the Statement of Faith: "God made human beings in His image that He might have fellowship with them. Being estranged from God by his disobedience, sinful human beings are incapable of a right relationship to God apart from divine grace."[29]

3) We proclaim the crucifixion of Jesus Christ as the ultimate proof of God's love and the only solution to our problem of sin.

The third proclamation begins with an assertion of Article V from the Young Life Statement of Faith—God's mercy and justice are evident at the cross in the manner in which Jesus died in our place, removing our guilt and reconciling us to God. Expanding upon this understanding, the third proclamation covers what Young Life is intending to do as they explain to young people what it means that "Jesus died for your sins." They desire to speak of Christ's sacrificial atonement and affirm that on the cross Christ:

> Demonstrated the love of God (Romans 5:8).
>
> Accomplished our reconciliation whereby our relationship with God is restored (Colossians 1:20–22; Ephesians 2:10).

29. Young Life, "Non-Negotiables," 4.

> Our sin is dealt with by redemption (Mark 10:45; Romans 3:24).
>
> Made propitiation or atonement for our sin (Romans 3:25).
>
> Provided for our justification (Romans 3:22-26).
>
> Conquered the power of Satan, evil, sin and death (Colossians 2:13-15; Colossians 1:13,14).
>
> Died as a substitute[30] for sinful humanity (Isaiah 53:5-6; II Corinthians 5:21)[31]

However, despite the variety of atonement theories presented and the plethora of Scripture passages given in support of their ideas of atonement, Young Life goes on to assert that on the Gospel accounts of Christ's death on the cross should be used when speaking on the crucifixion. They state, "Therefore, proclaiming the truth of the cross must center in the Gospel events of the crucifixion itself with other texts such as parables or selections from the Epistles or the Old Testament, etc., used only as secondary references."[32] They also emphasize that verbal proclamation should be the mode of communication about the death of Jesus rather than video representations in order to avoid emotionally manipulating young people into feeling sorry for Jesus. Emphasizing their understanding of Christ's death as substitutionary atonement, they assert video representations do not adequately explain Jesus' death as a substitutionary one.[33]

4) We proclaim the resurrection of Jesus Christ.

Young Life has written this proclamation (in such a way that they do not support their assertion) with a connection to the Statement of Faith.[34] They do, however, confess that adequate time is not often given for a clear procla-

---

30. Robert Webber notes that modern evangelism's focus on the substitutionary atonement of Christ is an important aspect in speaking about salvation. However, it does not encompass everything that must be said. "Its primary shortcoming is that it fails to move from the death of Christ to the victory of Christ over the powers of evil. Consequently, evangelism is reduced to personal and privatized Christianity . . . " (Webber, *Ancient-Future Faith*, 144).

31. Young Life, "Non-Negotiables."

32. Young Life, "Non-Negotiables," 5.

33. Ibid.

34. Proclamations four, five and six of the "Non-Negotiables" document are not directly supported by the Young Life "Statement of Faith."

mation and explanation of the resurrection within the ministry. They want to ensure that communication of the resurrection takes place in order to "communicate to kids that the resurrection validates the claims of Christ, illustrates God's triumph over sin, ensures that we, too, are now and will be resurrected to a new life. Jesus Christ is alive and lives in us today, imparting to us love, freedom, healing, identity, purpose, abundant and eternal life (John 10:10)."[35] Young Life desires to proclaim the good news of the resurrection in order to help young people realize they do not need to feel boxed in by their sin or by their position in life. They believe the passage from 1 John 4:4 can be true for young people as Christ's power is illustrated through the resurrection: "The one who is in you is greater than the one who is in the world."[36]

5) We proclaim the risen Christ's offer of salvation by inviting our high school, middle school and college friends to confess Jesus as Lord and Savior.

It is specifically under this point where theological debate has taken place within Young Life. Young Life states, "We proclaim the risen Christ's offer of salvation by inviting our high school, middle school, and college friends to confess Jesus as Lord and Savior."[37] Young Life believes that the gospel demands a response. "The sacrifice of Jesus, although sufficient for the salvation of the whole world, is only efficient for those who confess Jesus as Lord and respond in faith, appropriating Jesus' death and resurrection for themselves. We believe that only in responding in faith and repentance can Jesus' removal of sin and imparting of life begin."[38] Young Life wants to be clear that they are inviting young people to respond to a Living Christ—not to a religion or concept or idea. They desire to *invite* adolescent friends to make a decision or commitment to Christ because they believe Scriptures teach that people must embrace or respond to the Gospel in order to be saved. It is not their intention to create an environment where young people feel pressured to respond, or ostracized if they do not, but they still provide a non-manipulative opportunity for a public proclamation of faith.[39]

35. Young Life, "Non-Negotiables," 5.
36. Ibid.
37. Ibid., 1.
38. Ibid., 6.
39. The "Say-So" is an opportunity for young people to stand up and publicly testify to the rest of the camp what God has done for them. The name was originally taken from

But we are given a different perspective to the intention of Young Life through journal entries that were highlighted in the Summer 1994 issue of the Young Life magazine, *Relationships*. Through the journal entry presented (as expressed by Young Life itself) we are given a perspective of potential emotional manipulation. In an article titled, *"It'll be the Greatest Week in Your Life!"* journal entries written by a high school student from New York were presented in order to highlight the experience young people have at camp upon hearing the message about Jesus Christ for the first time. Focusing on entries from Day Four and Five of these entries we are able to see how Young Life sets up the message sequence at camp and how that might influence decisions taken by young people.

> Day Four:
>
> *Today was very depressing. We talked about the 10 commandments. I figured I had broken some of them, but not others like murder and adultery. The club speaker said murder isn't just taking a person's life. We can kill someone by ruining their reputation. He also said adultery isn't just the physical act. It includes feeling lustful towards someone. Man, I have broken every one of those commandments. He said if I have broken one of these commandments, I have broken God's heart. I wish that I could start over and never break one again. Doing that in today's society would be impossible . . .*
>
> Day Five:
>
> *This was the ultimate. Chuck talked about the purpose behind Jesus' crucifixion. God knew that Jesus would be sinless and would die on the cross. Through Jesus' death God is able to forgive all the sins that I've ever done. It's like a package that only has to be unwrapped. Jesus provides forgiveness for sins. I only have to receive it. After the talk, we were given 20 minutes to go out by ourselves and to think silently. Those 20 minutes felt like 5. I committed my life to Jesus Christ in that time. I asked Him to help me keep these thoughts forever. The emotions were overwhelming. I had never felt anything like it before.*[40]

From these anonymous journal entries we are able to see the emotional response to a carefully formed presentation of the Gospel. The breaking of the Ten Commandments, understood in culturally relevant ways like ruining someone's reputation or lusting, brings a sense of depression and need

---

Psalm 107:2 "Let the redeemed of the Lord say so, whom he hath redeemed from the hand of the enemy" (Sublett, *The Diaries of Jim Rayburn*, 285).

40. *Relationships*, Summer 1994, 21–22. Italics in original.

to start over in the eyes of God. The *next* day, then, a presentation is made about Christ's death on the cross and an invitation to accept Christ. Young people are encouraged to think deeply about this presentation when they are given twenty minutes of silence to consider the sacrifice of Christ. For young people, the twenty minutes of silent alone time was the moment a decision was made to dedicate one's life to Christ.

There have been other models proposed for the proclamation of Christ's work on the cross. Jeff McSwain argues for an alternative view to the work of Christ and its expression within Young Life. Within a document written by McSwain that preceded the gospel proclamation document of Young Life he states, "Jesus is the model for Young Life's foundational principle of incarnational with-ness. Jesus came near to sinners and was with them before and after their decisions to follow him. In the same way, Young Life leaders come near to 'sinners' and stick with them before and after their decisions to follow Christ."[41] McSwain centers his argument on Jesus being Immanuel, God with us. He argues that God in Jesus is with us both before and after any conversion to follow Christ. Therefore students would never be left with the perception like that presented above: depressed about the sinfulness and desire to start over with God, but left to wait a full day before they hear what Christ has already done on their behalf.

It is also under this fifth point, confession of Christ before you are saved, that other theologians from across the United States took offense when Young Life released their Non-Negotiable document.[42] Christian Smith of the University of Notre Dame and Doug Campbell of Duke Divinity School wrote a response to the Young Life document titled "Why the New Young Life 'Non-Negotiable' Statement on Gospel Proclamation Needs to be Re-considered." Smith and Campbell concluded that Young Life was taking a stance through this point of "repent and then you shall be saved."[43] They understood this to be conditional and sequential understanding of salvation that depended on human repentance and faith. This, in their view, was a type of "works righteousness" that does not reflect the sovereign love and grace of God.[44] They concluded that this was less a bibli-

---

41. McSwain, "Jesus Is the Gospel," 4.

42. Tony Jones, a theologian known for his work in the emerging church culture, concluded that this stance in the proclamation document was "shortsighted and shallow in the area of sotierology" (www.tonyj.net).

43. Smith and Campbell, "Why."

44. Ibid., 1.

cal position of salvation, and more a reflection of the American culture's "captivity to the rational choices of autonomous individuals to make contractual agreements as the basis of valid relationships."[45] They conclude that to make a suggestion that God had done nearly all the work of salvation *but* that teens need to fill in the last gap with their own confession and faith is "theologically misguided, organizationally parochial, and pastorally counter-productive in the subsequent discipleship of believing teens."[46]

6) We proclaim God's call to discipleship by encouraging all who respond to grow in their faith.

Under this final proclamation Young Life states their desire to produce disciples in the kingdom of God, not simply converts to the Christian faith. They desire to present to young people what it means to "follow Christ, be part of the church, and make a difference in the world." They consider being part of the body of Christ means you live out your faith with other believers, not living out an individualistic discipleship.[47]

Having established the six key points of proclaiming the gospel in Young Life, they include a specific outline for the sequence of talks that should be given within the Young Life organization. This sequence includes covering: the person of Jesus Christ (the overarching theme in all talks), the reality and consequence of sin (as explained before the crucifixion and resurrection), the truth about the crucifixion of Christ, the truth about the resurrection of Christ, the invitation that God extends, the call to discipleship, and the public proclamation of that response.[48] And they conclude their Non-Negotiable document by summarizing their intentions to claim responsibility for training staff and volunteer leaders in the proclamation of the Gospel. They are clear when they state:

> Once our staff and volunteers are trained, we will hold them accountable for the content and the clarity of our proclamation. We understand that there may be Young Life staff members or volunteers who would prefer to proclaim the Gospel in another way. But because the issue of how we proclaim the Good News of Jesus Christ to kids is at the heart of what we do and because we are

---

45. Ibid., 2.
46. Ibid., 2. Italics in original.
47. The issue of Bible study within Young Life will be discussed later in the chapter.
48. Young Life, "Non-Negotiables," 7.

called to be stewards of this high and holy responsibility, we will maintain our position as described in this paper.[49]

Young Life concludes the Non-Negotiable document by stating that they desire to be faithful followers of God, and that the ministry of Young Life is accomplished only by depending on God and His Spirit. Young Life desires to remain faithful to Scripture, and they base their understanding and this document on the truth they believe is contained within it.[50]

This, then, is an example of the belief that gave shape to Young Life from the early days. The resistance to intellectualize Christianity was a way in which to say they were much more comfortable with the practice of ministry they had already established. Although Young Life has, in the end, formulated statements of faith that they officially structure their ministry around, it is in fact the praxis of the ministry that sways their work. The methodology and the content of ministry of Young Life is first understood by the words of president Bill Starr as he articulated in 1968. Research revealed a letter from Starr to his board of directors in 1968.

A. The Definition of Young Life

This exercise has been essential in order to train others. Young Life has in a sense lacked definition, and because we live in a culture that is altering so rapidly, I thought we needed to begin this articulation. There are many ways in which this can be viewed, but I will take three:

Cultural

Young Life is an organization committed to penetrating the adolescent subculture in order to communicate the message of Christ. The key word is penetration.

Ingredients essential to penetration are:
- Involvement
- Identification
- Relationship

→ Adolescent Subculture

Theological

Young Life is a group of people bound together in a fellowship to expose the young people of our day to a Biblical incarnational Christology. The key word is exposure.

The boundaries are creative relationships on the one hand, and an attractive, intelligent non-judgmental articulation on the other. The basis is the Scripture.

— Definition of Young Life —
Incarnational   Christology
(Non-Verbal)   (Verbal)

Contact → Methodology → Content

Authority: Scripture

---

49. Ibid.
50. Ibid.

In this letter, Starr defines the theological underpinnings of Young Life. In a box in the lower right hand corner on the third page of the report he gives this description: "[The] definition of Young Life—incarnational (non-verbal) and Christology (verbal) with the authority of Scripture underneath it all. The non-verbal takes place through contact and the content through Christology. Contact leads to content through methodology."[51] To the side of this diagram, Starr explains that creative relationships form the boundary for the work, and articulation comes through an attractive, intelligent and nonjudgmental method. Forming the basis for all of this is Scripture.[52] After reviewing this letter and definition of the theological underpinning of Young Life, it became apparent that Young Life often begins with the practice of contact work and that, then, leads to a proclamation of the content of their faith. The practice of incarnational ministry precedes the articulation of Christological faith. The following portion of this chapter will articulate the manner in which Young Life understands incarnational witness, as well as the distinct doctrinal statements that are nuanced by the Young Life culture that permeates how they share Christianity with young people.

In some ways, Young Life understands the foundation from which they embody their faith. From a training manual (1969) the Young Life organization states:

> Though we have a system of beliefs, theologies and doctrines, historic evidences, even inspired Scriptures, we must proclaim that Christianity is CHRIST—Christ in us the hope of Glory. It is supremely a relationship to a Person, not a system, that we are to challenge kids to commitment. He is the center, the power, the dynamic, of our message; and He is alive, reigning, interceding, for us today.[53]

For the Young Life organization, the foundation of their ministry is the person of Christ rather than any specific articulation of what they understand of the person of Christ. It is the relational aspect of Christ that drives their understanding and their challenge of commitment to young people. And Starr sums up this understanding when he succinctly states, "For instance, I feel as though we have regained a sense of solid direction, and have seen

---

51. Starr, Letters 1968, 3.
52. Ibid.
53. Young Life, training manual, 6.

a deepening of the commitment on the part of our people to what has become the terms that describe us—Biblical, incarnational Christologists."[54]

The Young Life organization has articulated the starting point for their ministry is the methodology of contact work and the person of Christ. From this, practical belonging is inherent but theological belonging is not necessarily strongly understood. I agree with Anderson in that the praxis theology of evangelism was understood more quickly within the organization. I will now review the practical and theological starting point for Young Life ministry—incarnational theology.

---

54. Young Life, year-end report 1971, 1.

3

Incarnational Theology: Christology, Soteriology, Campaigners

I WAS A BASKETBALL player through my high school career. It was during my first, tumultuous year of high school that I recognized even in sports there could be difficulty. I had been moved to varsity as a freshman and though I was extremely honored and had a successful season, I experienced the isolation that can sometimes come with such a move. I was set apart from my classmates in the ninth grade because I was playing with the juniors and seniors. At the same time I was never quite accepted by the players on my team due to my age and was sometimes treated like the annoying little sister. In the middle of the season I received a note in the mail. My Young Life leader had seen my name in the newspaper after a win, and he jotted a quick note to let me know how proud he was of the team and me. Even though the note was short it made a deep impact and enabled me to see that the season wasn't just about me but about our community as a whole.

"The Young Life concept of a life-upon-life has been a distinguishing feature of our work. We go to kids to take love, recognition, acceptance, security, friendship, etc., in Christ's stead today. He lives in us to make this possible."[1] Young Life establishes its incarnational understanding not necessarily on theological grounds, but on the praxis of going to kids with the message of Christ. In a letter to the board of directors from Bill Starr, then executive director of Young Life, from December 1966, we find an explanation of Young Life's emphasis on Jesus-centered Christology. He states that Young Life is patterning their ministry after that of Jesus[2]: "Jesus went

---

1. Young Life, training manual, 11.
2. Andrew Root, in his book *Revisiting Relational Youth Ministry*, gives a similar

Incarnational Theology: Christology, Soteriology, Campaigners

where people were. He won their friendship, their interest. He built a bridge of sincere, meaningful relationship." Young Life staff people do similar things by going where young people are. "They [leaders] spend hours at ball games, at pizza parlors, in small groups, or with a lone teenager. They have one clear-cut purpose—to build a bridge of friendship. Face to face, person-to-person relationship is the heart of Young Life's ministry.... That is why Young Life concentrates on Christ. Its message is clear, uncluttered. Its one purpose is to bring the teenage person into informed, un-pressured, personal confrontation with Jesus Christ."[3]

But for the organization, it is the methodology of incarnation that prompts the efforts of the mission rather than the theological underpinnings that Christ's incarnation represents. Bill Starr stated:

> These factors produce an opportunity for Young Life to present a solution, a new possibility for them to consider. This is where the great idea of Incarnation comes in. This magnificent, awesome entrance of God into the human stream demonstrates how He feels about His own creation, about His own people and how He would handle us. I'd like to suggest that while we see the birth of Jesus Christ ranking at the top of all human history, we do not limit ourselves to talking a lot about the theology of incarnation–except as it forms a model for us. Rather, let us think of it as methodology.[4]

The incarnation, then, becomes a model for ministry that undergirds all of the work of Young Life as they seek to embody Christ for young people. As Christ came in to the world in the form of humanity, so Young Life seeks to enter into the world of teenagers, and they believe it is this commitment to incarnational life that distinguishes them from others. Starr again believed that the concept of a relational ministry was basic to Young Life ministry, and relational ministry came through earning the trust of young people through friendship. But Starr made distinctions between the relational aspect of ministry and the incarnational aspect of ministry. "In a day and age when the word 'relational,' and ideas regarding relationship are basic to any endeavor I think it's important to clearly distinguish between

---

explanation of Young Life's pattern. "Rayburn's theological justification for this approach to ministry is the incarnation of Jesus Christ. Because God, in the person of Jesus Christ, had entered a foreign cosmos to save it from destruction, so Rayburn (and Young Life leaders after him) entered a foreign world of youth culture to save it for Christ" (Root, *Revisiting Relational Youth Ministry*, 53).

3. Starr, Letter 1966, 1–3.

4. Starr, Letter 1973, 3.

what is *relational* and what is *incarnational*. By incarnational I mean that as individuals, we are insufficient to be all that we can be—without God. It is not simply a theological concept but a methodological idea as well. That is, we need the Holy Spirit to indwell in us, and to allow His love to live in us and through us."[5] Again Starr is emphasizing the methodological position of incarnation rather than the theological basis for it.

As Young Life seeks to embody the life of Christ through the prompting of the Holy Spirit, they have come to consider this being "Jesus with skin on." The Young Life training manual describes incarnational ministry like this: "Much has changed in 60 years . . . But two things remain the same. Kids still need adults who will step into their worlds with the love of Jesus Christ, and those adults still need to pray. Praying and going still constitute the crux of what has come to be called 'incarnational, relational ministry' in Young Life. Young Life leaders become 'Jesus with skin on' to lost and lonely kids."[6]

Young Life shapes their understanding of relationships in a specific way: it's a "party with a purpose." At the center of Young Life's new business card[7] you are given the four key concepts that guide the organization: out there, inviting, changed lives and a firm foundation.

OUT THERE	INVITING
Young Life goes into the world of kids, crossing barriers to build bridges of authentic friendship. We enter their world with no expectation of who kids should be, but with every hope for who they can become.	Young Life is like one big "party with a purpose" where all are welcome and treated like honored guests. It may be club – the best night of a kid's week; or camp – the best week of their life; or just the invitation to spend time with a leader who has become their friend. But before the party ends, we share a simple message about God's love for them.
• Young Life leaders are followers of Christ, called to kids.	• Young Life is about relationships.
• Young Life goes to kids, we don't ask them to come to us.	• Young Life is an experience of fun, adventure, grace and truth.
• Young Life is at home in the world of kids.	• In Young Life, we strive for excellence and exceed expectations.
• Young Life thinks kids are great and we want the best for each of them.	• Young Life is for every kid, regardless of ability, circumstance, race or culture.

5. Starr, Letter 1977, 2.

6. Young Life, leadership training manual, 59.

7. Young Life, business card. While in conversation with Terry Swenson, vice president of communication for Young Life, he described this as an "elevator card," a card to hand to someone who does not know what Young Life is (Field Journal, May 2008).

Incarnational Theology: Christology, Soteriology, Campaigners

CHANGED LIVES	FIRM FOUNDATION
Young Life believes that every adolescent deserves a chance to consider the Christian faith in terms they understand from people they trust. We encourage those who want to grow in their faith to explore it in study, deepen it in service, share it in leadership and celebrate it in a church of their choosing. And we respectfully continue to share our lives and message with those who choose otherwise, because our friendship and love in Christ come without conditions.	Young Life is making a difference in the lives of kids around the world because we are supported by adults who care about kids in their community; our staff and volunteer leaders are trained in time-tested methods of relating with adolescents; and we are equipped by a world-class organization dedicated to effective ministry.
• Young Life is for lost kids.	• Young Life has a long legacy of effective work with kids.
• Young Life shares the Gospel in an attractive way.	• Young Life has a wide reach, around the world and in every kind of community.
• In Young Life, we see kids' lives changed as they encounter Jesus Christ.	• Young Life has a reputation for excellence among adults who care about kids.
• Young Life challenges kids to take the next step in their faith.	• Young Life is positioned for ongoing growth.

Under the "inviting" heading you are met with this statement from the organization: "Young Life is like one big 'party with a purpose' where all are welcome and treated like honored guests. They understand this party to take place at either club ("the best night of a kid's week") or at camp ("the best week of their life").[8] "But before the party ends, we share a simple message about God's love for them." And these are two of the key phrases they share about their invitation to young people: Young Life is about relationships and Young Life is an experience of fun, adventure, grace and truth.[9] The Young Life relational and incarnational understanding of practical belonging is one of a party! The party is the vehicle for sharing the message of Christ, but it takes place after fun and adventure have happened. Young Life leaders are "out there" in order to "invite" young people to this party, and it is after this has taken place that the message of God is portrayed.

From the foundation of Jim Rayburn, Young Life established incarnational theology on building relationships with young people out of love. Rayburn followed the pattern of loving first in order to evangelize later. Young Life believes in following the example of Christ: going where the

---

8. "We in Young Life believe that how teens hear the message is as important as what they hear. Camping is our most effective expression of incarnational witness through mission community. The best way to make God's love visible is through a community of believers who care for each other so much they reach out to them with God's inclusive love . . . So far in Young Life, camping is our best expression of a community able to call others into relationship with their Creator" (*Relationships*, June/July 1987, 2).

9. Young Life, business card.

people are and being with them. Through the process of penetrating the youth subculture, Young Life developed this idea of incarnational theology through building relationships with teenagers on their ground, in their world. From this foundation Young Life establishes their doctrinal understanding on relational[10] concepts: A relationship with Christ is the most important relationship you could have, sin is the sign of a broken relationship with God, and Christ's crucifixion repairs our relationship with God through love, and discipleship is experienced more deeply in relationship. Loving relationships and Young Life's incarnational and relational theology become the foundation from which all doctrinal understanding takes place.

Christology of Young Life: Jesus-Centered Proclamation

I have just reviewed the foundational element of incarnational theology that shapes Young Life's understanding of the praxis of evangelism. However, through archival research and review of other documents produced by the organization, Young Life communicates conservative evangelical doctrine in a manner distinctive to their ministry. Christology, soteriology, ecclesiology, and discipleship are presented in ways that are central to the Young Life organization—focusing on Jesus Christ alone and from the perspective of relationships. From the beginning, the central focus of Jesus Christ in the ministry of Young Life was clearly articulated by Jim Rayburn. Rayburn, referencing his talk at a leadership-training seminar at Frontier Ranch[11] in an issue of the *Young Life* magazine, made note of two important things for Young Life:

> First, we must stick to presenting Jesus Christ. There are all kinds of secondary things we could get involved in, but they aren't Young Life's business. We are not to "major in the minors," but in the one all-important essential: Jesus Christ is our greatest need, and that He's all we need. He is far and away the most important and

---

10. I have purposely omitted the doctrine of ecclesiology from this specific list because the relational aspect of Young Life's understanding of church takes on a different tone from the other doctrinal concepts. I will consider the concept of ecclesiology more fully later in this chapter.

11. Frontier Ranch was one of the original camps established by Young Life.

Incarnational Theology: Christology, Soteriology, Campaigners

attractive person in the world and every high school fellow and girl needs to find that out. Second, we must love people.[12]

Young Life desires that young people have a clear picture of Christ's character, personality, power and love. They also acknowledge that the message of Young Life is Jesus. As noted above, they believe that every talk given within Young Life should center and spring from a gospel account of an event in the life of Jesus. They believe that salvation history has its origination and culmination in Jesus Christ, therefore all staff and volunteers should focus on clarifying the person of Jesus for young people.[13] The person of Jesus becomes the central point of every message of Young Life; and not only the central point: Young Life encourages Jesus to be the *only* message of Young Life. Bill Starr stated, "This is why we try in every way to introduce kids to the Person, not the Faith or to Christianity, but to Jesus Christ. We believe meeting Him is central to all the rest of living. The ultimate Friend. The supreme meaning that keeps life from being absurd."[14] This is the Christo-centric focus of the organization. Young Life leadership, in the Non-Negotiable document proclaims,

> We affirm Young Life's *style* is relational and incarnational. This means that our proclamation of the Gospel will almost always proceed from the context of relationships with adolescents. Our desire is to share not only the gospel of God, but our own lives as well. We believe this style of proclamation is both biblical and effective . . . However, while our *methodology* may change, our *message* does not.[15]

This language is also used in the October 1953 issue of the *Young Life* magazine. Rayburn states that friendliness is the "major" in Young Life. "There is a quality of friendliness and love that the Lord Jesus will put in our lives

---

12. *Young Life* magazine, October 1956, 20.
13. Young Life, "Non-Negotiables," 2.
14. Young Life, *Focus on Youth*, 3.
15. Young Life, "Non-Negotiables," 8. Emphases in original. Smith and Campbell believe this is the genius behind Young Life: real relationships with teenagers in real life. "That is sociologically brilliant, the way we know most faith conversions actually happen—and much more important than, say, the precisely sequenced order of thematic talks. The method very much is the message" (Smith and Campbell, "Why the New Young Life," 4).

if we will stay close to Him. And without it His work becomes fruitless and barren. Friendliness is our major in Young Life."[16]

The incarnational focus of Christ in the Young Life organization also originated with Jim Rayburn. Rayburn, in the February 1946 issue of the *Young Life* magazine stated:

> Christianity is fascinating. It is the most attractive message anyone has ever heard. I believe that can be proved. I'm not going to prove it in this little short column, but I am going to give you some potent reasons why Christianity is a plenty attractive proposition. Today I'll just mention the first and greatest reason—it is all based upon LOVE. The undying love of our great God and Savior for lost and sinful men is to every thinking person the finest story ever told.[17]

Rayburn bases his argument for love on the verse 1 John 4:10 as he stated in the March 1946 issue of the magazine. "Here is the real thing. Not that you have to love God so fervently that He will love you too. No, indeed!—far greater than that. The real truth of the matter is that long before you ever thought of loving God He loved you so much that He personally took care of all the terrible sin problem with its death and eternal penalty."[18] Rayburn's son, Jim Rayburn III, notes in his book *Dance Children Dance*, "To love starved young people, Jim sought to be a friend. Kids listened to Jim when they wouldn't listen to others because they knew he cared about them. And once he had built a bridge of friendship, he was naturally anxious to share the source of his love. Jim figured it is best to love first and save the evangelizing for later."[19] Through Rayburn's expression of the love of Christ, young people were made to feel the significance of their relationship with God–a relationship based on love.

Rayburn, in a letter from 1952, was explaining the work and mission of Young Life in this way: "We do have a very unique approach to the problem of reaching young people. You see we are after the UNREACHED . . . . The vast majority of young people are not in a church and never hear the truth about the Savior's love, so we are after them particularly. To reach them we have had to break with some traditional methods and, I am sorry to say, we

---

16. *Young Life* magazine, October 1953, 4.
17. *Young Life* magazine, February 1946, 3.
18. *Young Life* magazine, March 1946, 3.
19. Rayburn III, *Dance, Children, Dance*, 50.

have had to sometimes be misunderstood."[20] Rayburn goes on to explain "contact work"—the hours leaders spend with kids, meeting them where they are, going where they are. Time spent with young people forms Young Life into "more than an ordinary youth movement." Not only do they earn a hearing with young people, but also they stay with young people after they make a decision for Christ. Rayburn establishes this on the example of Jesus Christ. "The Lord Jesus Himself is our example in this. His heart was tender toward sinners. He longed for them. He was not ashamed to be with them. His compassionate approach to the lost is what we are after. We try to be kind in our approach to the lost." Rayburn insisted on gentleness and to honestly seek the Lord's guidance and to be as he was—"a friend of the publicans and sinners."[21]

Rayburn desired to form these relationships in order to share the love of Christ with young people. In the September 1945 issue of the *Young Life* magazine he states:

> If they do not know, they cannot believe. Say, Gang, that is really something. It is terrible, but it is true. I believe it. Only a very small portion of all the kids that you know even know what to believe about Jesus Christ. No wonder there are so many without Him. This makes me feel that the greatest job in the whole world for Christian young people in high school is to find some way to tell the gang about Jesus Christ—Who He is, and what He has done. We can never get them acquainted with Him until we get them to listen to the Word of God.[22]

Within the Young Life leadership-training manual their aim is described as "loving each kid to the Lord Jesus Christ." They do this through building a bridge of unconditional friendship that often "stretches from a concerned adult to an 'I-couldn't-care-less' adolescent."[23] They list ways to implement this plan through similar words of Rayburn and Starr: "winning the right to be heard, building a bridge of friendship and trust, understanding and

---

20. Young Life, leadership training manual, 16. Capitals in original.

21. Ibid.

22. *Young Life* magazine, September 1945, 3.

23. These words accompany the section in the leadership-training manual about preparation for contact work. "Acceptance by kids depends primarily upon our love for them and our ability to communicate this love non-verbally and verbally. But physical appearance and health should be carefully observed. First impressions are often formed by physical appearance" (Young Life, leadership training manual, 62).

penetrating a culture, and demonstrating Christ's love."[24] They conclude by saying this process is ongoing, but Young Life believes with Christ living within humanity the incarnation is still in process today.[25]

As I have shown, an emphasis on the person of Christ is the central focus of the Young Life organization and their proclamation of the gospel. They believe that the message of Christ is best understood through genuine, caring relationships built between adults and teenagers, and that the message of Christ will remain as the driving force behind the organization. I will now review the message of sin and salvation as presented by Young Life and the distinctive manner in which it is presented in relational terms.

Soteriology of Young Life: Sin and Salvation through Relationships

Sin

I have just reviewed the doctrine of Christology as presented by Young Life through various documents, and the central focus of Christ in every aspect of the organization. Young Life places emphasis on the priority of the message of Christ and the model of Christ's life framing the belief and work of the organization. Young Life also utilizes a language of love and relationship to describe sin and the crucifixion of Christ. In order to highlight the emphasis, I return to the words of the Non-Negotiable document. In their Non-Negotiable document, Young Life describes the issue and reality of sin as a broken relationship with God. They use relational words to describe the issue of sin: estrangement, alienation, lost-ness, and purposelessness. The document also continues, "We also maintain that words such as *guilty, rebellious, separated,* and *condemned* are descriptions that characterize sinful humanity and necessitate God's ultimate rescue in the person of Jesus Christ."[26] God rescues us through Jesus Christ by "His presence and His pursuit 'while we were yet sinners'—that leads us to repentance, turning from life on our own apart from God to life in relationship with God through Jesus Christ. Young Life notes that 'we are not *hopeless* because of the love of God in Jesus Christ, but we are *helpless* to make things right on our own'"[27]

24. Ibid., 61.
25. Ibid.
26. Young Life, "Non-Negotiables," 3.
27. Ibid., 4. Emphases in original. Rayburn reminds readers in the March 1951 issue

INCARNATIONAL THEOLOGY: CHRISTOLOGY, SOTERIOLOGY, CAMPAIGNERS

The proof of God's love is found in the crucifixion of Christ on the cross. Young Life senior leaders, under the third point of the Non-Negotiable document, state that the only solution to the problem of sin is the crucifixion of Jesus Christ. They affirm that on the cross, Jesus: "Demonstrated the love of God, accomplished reconciliation, dealt with sin by redemption, made atonement for sin, provided our justification, conquered the power of Satan, and died as a substitute for sinful humanity."[28] Young Life, therefore, takes on a traditional substitutionary view of Christ's redemption of humanity through his death on the cross.[29] Because Christ died on our behalf-became our substitute-we obtain salvation through our belief in him. They explain that the key texts used for proclaiming the cross should be crucifixion narratives found in the gospels. "Therefore, proclaiming the truth of the cross must center in the Gospel events of the crucifixion itself with other texts such as parables or selections from the Epistles or the Old Testament, etc., used only as secondary references."[30] Young Life believes verbally proclaiming the accounts of the gospel is preferred over video representation because video representations often play on emotions and do not adequately portray Jesus as our substitute. "Because of that, the crucifixion narrative as stated in the Gospels will be our main text

---

of the *Young Life* magazine of what they did when they became Christians. "First of all, you realized your utter helplessness. Your goodness wasn't fit for God. Then you discovered the price Christ paid to make you right with God. And, finally, you trusted in Him as your personal Savior" (*Young Life* magazine, March 1951, 4).

28. Young Life, "Non-Negotiables," 5. Rayburn also made note of theological categories in the February 1957 edition of the *Young Life* magazine. He listed five "big words of the Christian faith. 1. Reconciled 2. Redeemed 3. Regenerated 4. Propitiated 5. Sanctified" (*Young Life* magazine, February 1957, 19).

29. Young Life often uses the "bridge illustration" to explain this concept. Whether through a conversation using a drawing or with props during a camp talk, the bridge illustration shows the chasm between God and people that can only be "bridged" through the cross of Christ. It was an illustration given to me as a high school student (see Appendix) and is still utilized by leaders today to explain Christianity to students. In an article about reaching high school students for Christ Elaine Carpenter recounted her interaction with two girls: "OK, let me make it simple and show you something really cool, then you can ask me questions as we go if you still have trouble understanding. And that's when I showed them the bridge illustration (a visual tool that helps explain the Gospel)–which became a conversation where they could fill in just about everything!" (*Relationships*, Spring 2009, 6).

30. Young Life, "Non-Negotiables," 5.

in proclaiming Jesus' work on the cross."[31] Rayburn himself utilized John chapters 18 and 19 for his explanation of the crucifixion:

> Did you know that they whipped him (19:1), that they ridiculed him and slapped him around (19:2–3), that they spit in his face, and finally spiked him to a wooden cross and left him to die? The picture of physical suffering should move us out in love and appreciation to the place where we could do nothing else but accept him as our own.[32]

Salvation

As we have seen in the previous section, sin, according to Young Life, is separation from a relationship with God. Our relationship with God can only be transformed through believing in the substitutionary work of Christ on the cross. Salvation[33] within Young Life, then, becomes a transformed life that exhibits the joy found in a growing relationship with Christ. Jim Rayburn was clear, in the early days of the ministry of Young Life, in his understanding of abundant life.[34] Within the first year of printing the *Young Life* magazine, Rayburn reflected in his "Say, Gang" editorial piece that they desired the magazine to be attractive and full of life. This was in an effort to express the full life Jesus Christ offered to young people. Rayburn stated that Jesus was the most fascinating person in the universe and would captivate the heart of any young person who knows Him. Jesus is "attractive—the only One Who is completely that! He is full of life—an abundance

---

31. Ibid.

32. *Young Life* magazine, July 1951, 4.

33. Just before his death, Jim Rayburn handed an envelope to Bob Mitchell with important terms of salvation that Rayburn considered the most important. "The Finished Work of Christ were written and underneath were the words 'forgiveness,' 'redemption,' 'propitiation,' 'sanctification,' 'justification,' and a few other theological terms related to salvation that Rayburn had studied under Dr. Chafer at Dallas Theological Seminary over thirty years before. He handed the envelope to Mitchell with a smile and said, "*That's what we're all about!*" (Sublett 2008, p. 503).

34. In a manual for Young Life skits, the introduction reads, "The Abundant Life is promised to us all. Fun, laughter, and hilarious entertainment are surely one part of that exciting Christian life. Fun breaks the ice, makes new kids feel relaxed, takes the stuffed-shirt feel out of Christianity, communicates our joy and gives even the shyest attender a reason to invite a friend to come with him next week" (Skits volume 1, Debbie-Jo White circ. 1976).

of it! Are you enjoying life in abundance? God's Word says that He came that we might have life, and that we might have it more abundantly. God is the only one Who could make such a promise to you."[35] Rayburn believed a Christian's life was one that was different. "Instead of life growing less like we want life to be, *it becomes more the life that really clicks.* Christians are the only people in the world who can experience this wonderful treasure—life getting better forever after. That is one of the little things we get when we get Jesus Christ."[36] The understanding of salvation within Young Life from the early days, then, is that a life begins to get better and better and "clicks" for those who "get Christ."

The following year, Rayburn, in his "Say, Gang" piece titled "There's a Big Lie Going Around," emphasizes the attractive life Christ has to offer. Rayburn emphasizes his argument using capital letters and italics in his piece:

> There's a big *lie* going around. It makes me *mad* every time I hear it—and I've heard it plenty lately. The thing that bothers me is it is such a smart, crafty life that it is making fools out of some of the swellest kids I know. Here it is: "CHRISTIANITY IS DULL." Oh, it takes many different forms. Sometimes it's "THE BIBLE IS OLD FOGEY. YOU CAN'T BE BOTHERED WITH THAT!" or "YOU HAVEN'T TIME FOR THAT STUFF, YOU GOTTA LIVE!" But always it is the same general idea—Christianity and the things that go with it are dull, boring, lifeless, unimportant. And I say *that's a lie—a lie so big that only the Devil could have started it.*[37]

Rayburn concludes stating the Christian faith is the most attractive proposition in the whole world and that those who know Christ should announce that message with all of their energy.[38]

Rayburn illustrates the characteristics of life you might receive when you accept Christ. "If you'll trust [God] each day, He'll give you strength, and wisdom, and courage, and victory over sin—everything you need to come out on top, everything you don't have yourself, everything that He has available to you in His big storehouse of resources for the Christian."[39] And Rayburn believed Young Life was an outgrowth of the conviction that

35. *Young Life* magazine, March 1945, 2.
36. *Young Life* magazine, June 1948, 4. Emphases in original.
37. *Young Life* magazine, February 1946, 3.
38. *Young Life* magazine, February 1946, 3.
39. *Young Life* magazine, February 1951, 4.

Jesus is all kids want most—"the most wonderful, the most attractive, the strongest, most gracious, loving person this world has ever seen."[40] And finally, in the May 1955 issue of the *Young Life* magazine, Rayburn puts it into language young people could relate to. "First, it's true that anything that's right to do we can do better with the Lord Jesus than without. He can make you a friendlier person, a better athlete, a better student than you could possibly be alone . . . . He has a wonderful plan for your life, if you're a Christian."[41] Salvation becomes a manner in which young people can become better than what they perceive themselves to be on their own. Young Life presents salvation not as theological tenets to believe, but what a life might look like after salvation takes place.

Even so, Young Life has simplified the steps[42] for salvation into a prayer of ABCs. In their discipleship handbook titled *Young Life Road Trip: a Journey Along the Road to Real with your Friends*[43] from 2007, they state:

> It's as simple as A-B-C, Admit, Believe, Commit.[44] Here's a prayer that can help you make the change: *God, I admit that I've been going the wrong way, walking away from you, living life on my own. I believe that you have provided forgiveness and eternal life through Jesus Christ. I commit to turning around in my tracks today to follow Him. I can't do this on my own, God. I will need you to give me your strength each step of this journey. Thank you for loving*

---

40. *Young Life* magazine, November 1953, 4.

41. *Young Life* magazine, May 1955, 4.

42. Rayburn reminds readers in the March 1951 issue of the *Young Life* magazine of what they did when they became Christians. "First of all, you realized your utter helplessness. Your goodness wasn't fit for God. Then you discovered the price Christ paid to make you right with God. And, finally, you trusted in Him as your personal Savior" (*Young Life* magazine, March 1951, 4).

43. The discipleship handbook notes this about your personal road trip: "There is something unique about your road trip with Jesus, however. You aren't traveling in a car. It's more like you're moving along life's highway in an RV. Jesus has made His home within you through the presence of his Holy Spirit. YOU are God's mobile home!" (Young Life, *Road Trip*, 35).

44. In an article about leading two high school students to faith, Young Life leader Elaine Carpenter reports on this interaction with the students. "Belky and Norma were so excited to see all this as real—that they could have a relationship with God and experience eternal life—and it was something they could understand and were free to do on their own! Once they understood the process of admitting, believing and committing their lives to God, Belky looked me in the eye and said, 'How can I start living this now?'" (*Relationships*, Spring 2009, 6).

me, for rescuing me and for putting my feet on the road to real life. Amen.[45]

Salvation, then, according to the organization, is admitting, believing, and committing your life to Christ, but salvation does not include theological tenets to assent to intellectually. Rather, salvation becomes a vision of what a transformed life in Christ might look like. With Christ, your life will become a life of strength, wisdom, and victory over sin—everything you need to have a life of top quality. As Rayburn stated, you'll be a better student, athlete, and friendlier person through salvation in Jesus.

As young people commit their lives to Christ through this Christocentric proclamation and guarantee of transformed life through salvation, Young Life has stated their intention of deepening the relationship the young person has with Christ through discipleship. In the following section I highlight the relational aspect Young Life emphasizes in fostering discipleship and the distinct manner in which they articulate that understanding.

Campaigners: A Model of Discipleship for Young Life

In this section I review the ministry of Campaigners and what Young Life believes about discipleship with young people who have made a commitment to Christ. This model of discipleship has been present in the ministry from early on,[46] but continues to take on culturally relevant forms in terms of their relational understanding. Discipleship is about your relationship with Christ, how Christianity affects your relationships, and being on the journey in relationship to your peers or leader. Discipleship is relationship.

Denny Rydberg, current president of Young Life, articulates an understanding of what the organization believes discipleship is all about.

> Those of us in Young Life stand on the bank of life's river fishing for adolescents. The place where we fish is rocky and turbulent but the catch is good. And like most good fly fishermen, after the catch we release them to a life of service to Jesus Christ. But it's how we release them that matters. Our desire is to release them in better

45. Young Life, *Road Trip*, 15.

46. Sublett notes that it was Dawson Trotman of the Navigators who encouraged Rayburn to put an emphasis on "follow up" with students who became Christians through Young Life. It was around 1942 that Young Life then began their Campaigners discipleship program using Navigator material (Sublett, *Diaries of Jim Rayburn*, 100).

shape than we found them. Before they are released, we help these kids better understand what it means to be life-long followers of Jesus Christ. We help them discover what it means to be His disciple. The Lord is the Master Discipler. God uses a variety of people and experiences to disciple His catch. A young person who gives his or her life to Christ at a camp or club or through a conversation with a peer or an adult may develop a special relationship with one person and that person may play a key role in discipleship. Great. But the Lord also uses a team of people to disciple someone. The team might include some peers. Add to the mix a parent or two, some Young Life leaders, a pastor, a teacher at school who is a believer. And the critical players may even change from year to year in the life of this new disciple because discipleship is a lifelong process and not a single event . . . That's discipleship and that's what Young Life is all about. Catch and release.[47]

Kit Sublett, in the Young Life leadership manual, notes that historically within the Young Life organization Christian students were encouraged to pray for their non-Christian friends this became the foundation for Campaigners, the name given to those who had given their lives to Christ and began a life of discipleship. As Sublett notes, Campaigners came from the original name of the Young Life ministry (the Young Life Campaign) so it was natural to call those who were very involved in the ministry "Campaigners."[48] As Young Life began having success in reaching disinterested students, staff began to realize the need for a discipleship program that would encourage new Christians on their journey as well as give ownership to Christian students[49] in the life of their school. Because of the friendship between Jim Rayburn and Dawson Trotman of the Navigators, the Navigators instructed Young Life on discipleship methods and gave Young Life training materials for discipling new believers.[50]

A disciple, according to Young Life, is a person who has invited Christ into their heart and desires to love Christ with all that they have. A disciple is a follower and a learner—one who desires first and foremost to love God and please him in all things. Linking discipleship to relationships, they go

47. *Relationships*, Fall 1993, 3–4.

48. Young Life, training manual, 84.

49. In 1987 Doug Burleigh stated, "Christian kids play a key role in the Young Life club—bringing their friends and praying for them as they consider Christ—but we do not desire to compete with the church for their time. We trust the Holy Spirit's directing them on their personal journey of faith" (*Relationships*, August 1987, 2).

50. Young Life, training manual.

INCARNATIONAL THEOLOGY: CHRISTOLOGY, SOTERIOLOGY, CAMPAIGNERS

on to state that a disciple is a person who has Jesus in the number one position in their life, "including the all-important area of relationships." They ask questions pertaining to the centrality of Christ in various relationships: boyfriend or girlfriend, the Lordship of Christ in your family, and the position of Christ in relation to yourself. They conclude with this question, "If you desire to get your relationships squared away, how can you proceed? How can Christ help you? How can the fellowship assist?"[51]

A description of the Campaigners program as given by president Doug Burleigh in 1987 is twofold: a connection to a small group study within Campaigners and a connection with the local church. Burleigh describes the Campaigner program this way: "Our vision for the Campaigners discipleship programs majors on personal spiritual disciplines. These include regular devotional times in the Scriptures, Bible memory and a growing prayer life. The fellowship of a small Campaigners group fosters informal accountability and mutual encouragement in developing such disciplines."[52] Burleigh goes on to note that though the Bible is often the focus of study for Campaigner groups, topics for study might also include issues concerning family, friends, drugs, sex and dating, or the church. The purpose of a Campaigner group is to form a safe environment where questions can be asked and fellowship established with peers seeking to follow God with their lives.[53]

In a manuscript titled *Road Trip: A Journey Along the Road to Real with Your Friends* (2007), Young Life established a seven-week discipleship course for new Christians. The intention of the study was to be done in relationship with others. They state:

> Also, you'll need *FRIENDS!* Yes, that's right, COMPADRES, HOMIES, whatever—you get the point. Friends aren't absolutely necessary for this road trip, but they will make it much more fun . . . Oh, we almost forgot. Did we mention your *YOUNG LIFE LEADER?!* Best case scenario: you work through your personal copy of the Young Life Road Trip on your own each day, then you

---

51. Young Life, training manual, 33–36. The discipleship training manual *Grow! Young Life Studies in Basic Christianity* does not include a specific copyright date. However, in the introductory remarks it notes that Young Life has been operating for thirty-five years, thereby dating this manual to the era around 1976.

52. *Relationships*, August 1987, 2.

53. Ibid.

meet with your friends and your Young Life leader once a week to share the ride!⁵⁴

At the conclusion of this training manual, Young Life reminds new disciples that relationships with peers and leaders encourages a close relationship with Christ: friends who follow Jesus, a small group who will study God's word, an adult mentor who will lend encouragement along the way, and a close connection with a local church.⁵⁵ Discipleship is relational in nature at all levels according to the praxis of Young Life.

An illustration of what takes place at a Campaigners meeting was given in the Summer 2000 edition of *Relationships*. Highlighting the volunteer work of Lee and Helen Gilliatt of Shelby, North Carolina, the article noted the work that goes into a typical Friday morning Campaigners meeting hosted by the Gilliatts. This Campaigner group started in the 1980s when a group of young men would meet at the local donut shop, but before long the group became co-ed and breakfast moved from the donut shop to the home of the Gilliats. Helen cooks for an average of forty-five students every week, and her menu includes eggs, grits, homemade pop tarts or honeybun cake. Breakfast begins at 7 a.m. and after they finish eating, students listen to Lee give a twenty-five minute lesson on the Bible—this article noted they were studying the book of Matthew for the entire school year.⁵⁶

In the following section I will present two differing views of the church that are apparent through the Young Life organization: a tenuous relationship with the Church because of misunderstood intentions, and a working relationship established with the Church through the Young Life church partnership agreement. Young Life believes in a commitment to connecting young people to the Church once a relationship with Christ is established. However, over the years, the application of this belief has often been lacking because of the fragile relationship between the organization and the Church. In the following section I will note the historic perspective on the relationship with the Church as well as show how partnerships between Young Life and the Church were established in order to share the message of Christ with as many young people as possible. I believe that Young Life holds a love/hate relationship with the Church.

---

54. Young Life, *Road Trip*, 1. Emphases and capitals in original.
55. Young Life, training manual, 116.
56. *Relationships*, Summer 2000, 11.

INCARNATIONAL THEOLOGY: CHRISTOLOGY, SOTERIOLOGY, CAMPAIGNERS

Young Life and the Church: An Ecclesiological Tug of War

In the previous section I discussed the effort of Young Life to encourage discipleship in young people who made a commitment to Christ through the ministry of the organization. In the midst of the discipleship program, Young Life also encourages young people to participate in and join a church where they feel comfortable as part of their discipleship process. However, there has been a difficult history between the Church and Young Life over the years—beginning with the experience and attitude of founder Jim Rayburn.

In the previous chapter on history, I noted the attitude of Rayburn towards the institutional church: Rayburn established his position by stating, "I am identified with the modern institutional church. I am a member of one of the most institutional of them all, a Presbyterian minister in good standing in my presbytery for twenty-one years. Quite a record for a fellow in my line of work. The Presbyterians frown on anything they can't control, and I'll give you a clue: they can't control me. I am identified, and I trust loyally so and constructively so, with the local, organized church."[57] Within this statement it is possible to grasp the frustrated and tenuous relationship Rayburn had with the institutional church, and the fragile relationship between Rayburn and the Church would extend over many years.

In this address to Young Life staff in the official staff letter titled *Monday Morning*, Rayburn illustrates the polar ends of his understanding and relationship with the church. Rayburn was describing the response churches had after attending meetings with staff person John Miller for the purpose of establishing contact with and informing churches of the purpose and mission of Young Life. Rayburn notes there was a positive response from the Mennonite church of Kansas and other cordial friendships that were established because of those meetings. But he goes on to state, "A number of such contacts recently have impressed upon me the great importance of developing broad contacts among the evangelical men in small denominational groups. Almost invariably these people are not as denominationally minded and not as sectarian in spirit as many of the leaders in the large denominations today . . . . Even more important, many of their people are warm-hearted, praying Christians and to have them informed about Young

---

57. Rayburn III, *Dance, Children, Dance*, 137.

Life would certainly add to our spiritual and material support."[58] The attitude of Rayburn was one of welcoming those churches that aligned with his understanding of Christianity and believed their support would add to the ministry of Young Life, but those who attacked the work and ministry of Young Life remained a frustration for the founder. However, at the end of the article in *Monday Morning*, Rayburn illustrates the contrasting nature of his relationship with the Church—heartily welcoming and highlighting the support of an institutional church. "During the past week we have received gifts from six different Presbyterian church benevolence budgets totaling $1200. I thought you would be interested in that little item that I just happened to notice from the receipts."[59]

However, the polarized attitude of Rayburn and the Young Life organization could be justified because of the attacks they felt were launched at them from the institutional church. In a *Time* magazine article from January 1960 it is reported that five leading Protestant ministers publicly rebuked Young Life for their practice and their message. "Young Life is, in effect, a separate teenage church, financed and directed by adults who are not answerable to any local group. We believe its outlook is too narrow, and that its emotional effect is eventually damaging to the young people most attracted by its appeal. The leaders tend in the direction of fundamentalism. They give easy answers to life's most difficult problems."[60]

Towards the end of his tenure as president of Young Life, Rayburn organized a meeting of mainline denominational leaders in an effort to explain and express the work of Young Life and the cooperation Rayburn believed could benefit both sides. However, the strength of Rayburn's opinion might have done more harm than good when he stated:

> It will be a fine thing if, a few years from now when the Rayburn plan is official in the denominations, that you fellows won't have to hire any more unqualified flunkies.... I go to churches where, instead of focusing on worship, half the service seems to be announcing the youth groups and where each one is going to meet. I don't know where we got so off the track. Yes I do, I have been around a lot of denomination headquarters.[61]

58. Rayburn, *Monday Morning*.
59. Ibid.
60. *Time*, January 1960, 54-55.
61. Rayburn, Chicago Fellowship transcript, 63.

Incarnational Theology: Christology, Soteriology, Campaigners

Rayburn also gave advice to the gathered leaders by trying to simplify their work with young people by advising pastors to focus on the worship service rather than the "extra-curricular" activities of youth work. Rayburn believed that, from his meditation and contact with young people, the church should be one of New Testament emphasis—being a family of the redeemed with the purpose of worship and instruction.[62]

Jim Rayburn III believed his father grew concerned later in life that thousands of young people who were new to the Christian faith and overflowing with joy and excitement had nowhere to go to experience a New Testament type of faith. "To plug those kids into a stiff religious system was to slowly snuff out the excitement and joy of walking with the Lord Jesus Christ. Jesus cannot be found in dry and boring religious environments. More often than not joining the mainline religious establishment is the kiss of death to any excitement a new believer may be experiencing."[63]

I have highlighted the contentious relationship that Rayburn and the Church had in the early days of the Young Life organization. There were attacks launched by some pastoral leaders to discredit Young Life, and there were also efforts on behalf of Young Life to attempt to repair those relationships. As time progressed, the tenuousness of the relationship between the two bodies eased to the extent they were able to see the benefits of working with one another in an effort to reach young people for Christ. Bill Starr stated in his annual report of 1970,

> In the past few years we have received less opposition from the institutional church than ever in our history. This is probably due to the honesty of the church leaders in acknowledging the fact that there has been general failure in church outreach to un-churched kids ... A big challenge faces us as we think of what contribution we might make to the church ... Other churches are asking Young Life for specific help in their programs and philosophy. It seems that we should gear up to meet these needs more adequately.[64]

Acknowledging the ecclesiology of gifts and benefits, a working relationship evolved between Young Life and the institutional church. Young Life believed the institutional church was finally looking to them for help in reaching teenagers, and I believe Young Life was recognizing the benefits of the institutional church for providing discipleship for young people as

62. Ibid., 61.
63. Rayburn III, *Dance, Children, Dance*, 148.
64. Young Life, year-end report 1970-1971, 8.

well as some professional clout to their organization. The following sections provide specific examples that bear out my beliefs.

Church Partnerships

One way in which Young Life and the institutional church became partners in ministry evolved through what is now called church partnerships. Beginning in the 1970s, Young Life leaders found themselves working on behalf of the organization as well as being supported by local churches. An early observation was made that it could be a win-win situation for both groups: Young Life would offer their method and philosophy of youth ministry to those working in the Church, and a church would benefit from the Young Life leader bringing in un-churched kids to their congregation. Charlie Scott, an early church partner in Young Life, noted the foundation for his work in establishing relationships between Young Life kids and the Church: "One of my great frustrations was that the kids who met Christ at Young Life camps rarely, if ever, made any significant connection with churches right after their commitment."[65] Scott began to understand the reasons why young people were not making the transition to church after becoming believers. The activities that comprise the process of building relationships with young people, walking with them, encouraging a faith in Christ all included the Young Life leader. However, once the decision to follow Christ had been made it was impossible for the leader to accompany every individual believer to church. "Everybody wins through church partnership. The church wins because they have well-trained, enthusiastic youth leaders working with their junior and senior high students. Young Life wins because the church provides a strong and stable volunteer to lead a local Young Life club in the high school where most of those church kids attend."[66]

Scott also observed that churches were recognizing the benefit of Young Life in the way in which they were reaching young people that the Church wasn't. In Scott's Young Life club there was a combination of kids that attended church and those who had not previously attended church but were doing so now because of the ministerial partnership between Young Life and the local church. Scott believed churches were finally understanding the attitude that Young Life held: "It is evidently apparent that we mean it when we say, 'We would be happy to work our way out of a job

---

65. Young Life, *Reaching Out*, 18.
66. Ibid., 19.

with Young Life. We would hope that the churches will be doing such a great job reaching outsiders that Young Life will no longer have to exist.' This we believe and this we proclaim in central Florida."[67]

Yet through my research, I came across longstanding attitudes when it came to the relationship between the Church and Young Life ministry. When I asked a long time staff member why Young Life had established within the constitution that the organization would only operate for fifty years he answered, "Because we thought the Church would have caught on by then, and they haven't" (Personal conversation during field research in Colorado Springs, Summer 2005, Field journal). And there was a similar sentiment expressed to me in a conversation I held with a local Young Life leader. Henry[68] said to me, "If the Church could catch on and start doing this relational thing, but they just haven't. They haven't caught on yet."[69] There remains an attitude of frustration amidst the Young Life organization when it comes to the institutional church not carrying the enthusiasm and relational aspect of ministry with young people.

Yet positive elements remain on the both the part of the Church as well as Young Life. A pastor in a local Presbyterian church stated:

> Young Life has deeply affected our church as well as the Christian life in our community. It is the same gospel, unafraid to be contemporary, spontaneous, and individual. And as with our Easter group, the leader speaks less and everybody else comes on more. Our church has become more welcoming, more tolerant of dress and looks. Their sympathies and understanding are awakened to "even these least ones" as well as the stranger and the odd ball. The church's cross-fertilization also blesses Young Lifers. After all, Christianity is not a sect with hair restrictions in either extreme, and the guitar is no more or less sacred than the organ. If the church is really the church, it has room for old Franciscans, black Quakers, Jesus Freaks, Catholic Pentecostals and Chinese Dutch Reformed junior highs.[70]

And Young Life emphasizes the familial and relational aspect that young people can find in the church once they make a commitment to Christ. They state that although young people might have not considered church

---

67. Young Life, *Focus on Youth*, Summer 1972, 21.
68. The name has been changed to protect identity.
69. Field journal: 4 March 2009.
70. Young Life, *Focus on Youth*, Summer 1974, 10.

an appealing or exciting part of life before making a commitment to Christ, that element can change.

> Most attend church for something they intend to *get* from it. However, church is not meant for you to get as much as it is meant for you to *give*. In church we give honor, worship, praise, prayers and service as we grow in our love for Jesus and His people. We now have a place where we belong. In church we also discover that God has a lot of friends. They come in all shapes, colors and sizes. Church is far more than a club for people your age. It's a family–with babies, kids, aunts, uncles, grandparents and all the in-laws. In this family we get to live out our love for all different kinds of people.[71]

Further, Young Life includes this prayer in their discipleship handbook to express their understanding of church. Using the symbol of refreshing waters that nurture our spirit they say, "And when I combine my river with the rivers of others who know you, we can create a great roar! Father, I ask that you would give me good opportunities to worship you with others. Help me to take the opportunity—to make the opportunity—by becoming an active part of your family in a local church."[72]

The doctrinal foundations of Young Life as considered in the theological terms of Christology, soteriology, discipleship and ecclesiology are all based on the incarnational witness of relationships. Young Life gives distinct voice to their understanding of these theological terms and presents them in a way distinctive to their ministry. Young Life was often more interested in the methodological position of the organization rather than the theological positioning for such ministry. However, Young Life also articulated their theological statements of faith even though it was a process that took place later in their organizational life as compared to other evangelical youth ministries.

The Drawbacks of Loose Theology

I began my archival research in the summer of 2005, and then, remarkably, Young Life as an organization entered a season of theological discussion because of a disagreement about what content could be part of the proclamation within a Young Life club. The disagreement led to the severance of

71. Young Life, *Road Trip*, xx-xxi.
72. Ibid., 95.

employment for a Young Life area director in North Carolina. Over some months of 2007, then, the Young Life organization found themselves in a season of theological reflection in efforts to clearly articulate what they believe, how to relate that to young people, and why it is important for staff and volunteers of Young Life. The national Young Life office released a document titled "Non-Negotiables of Young Life's Gospel Proclamation" in October 2007 (Received via email, November 2007). This document, written by senior leaders within the organization, set out to provide "direction and clarity" for what and how the gospel is proclaimed throughout the organization.[73] This document outlines and then expands six points that give guidance to the content and the practice of proclaiming the gospel of Christ within the ministry of Young Life. To review, Young Life establishes these six points as non-negotiable for their gospel proclamation: they proclaim the person of Jesus Christ, they proclaim the reality of sin and its consequences—apart from divine grace we are estranged from God, they proclaim the crucifixion as the ultimate proof of God's love, they proclaim the resurrection of Christ, they proclaim Christ's offer of salvation by inviting Young Life young people to confess Jesus as Lord and Savior, and finally, they proclaim God's call to discipleship by encouraging growth in faith.[74]

It is specifically under point number five where theological debate has taken place. Young Life states, "We proclaim the risen Christ's offer of salvation by inviting our high school, middle school, and college friends to confess Jesus as Lord and Savior."[75] Young Life believes that the gospel demands a response. "The sacrifice of Jesus, although sufficient for the salvation of the whole world, is only efficient for those who confess Jesus as Lord and respond in faith, appropriating Jesus' death and resurrection for themselves. We believe that only in responding in faith and repentance can Jesus' removal of sin and imparting of life begin."[76] However, Jeff McSwain, a former area director for Young Life in North Carolina, argues for an alternative view to the work of Christ and its expression within Young Life. Within a document written by McSwain—one that preceded the gospel proclamation document of Young Life—he states, "Jesus is the model for Young Life's foundational

73. Young Life, "Non-Negotiables," 1. Terry Swenson, vice-president of communication for Young Life, notes, "There's a practical element to this that drives a lot of what we're attempting to do" (Hansen, "Gospel Talk").

74. Young Life, "Non-Negotiables," 1.

75. Ibid.

76. Ibid., 6.

principle of incarnational with-ness. Jesus came near to sinners and was with them before and after their decisions to follow him. In the same way, Young Life leaders come near to 'sinners' and stick with them before and after their decisions to follow Christ."[77] McSwain centers his argument on Jesus being Immanuel—God with us. He argues that God in Jesus is with us both before and after any conversion to follow Christ.

It is also under this fifth point—confession of Christ before you are saved—that other theologians from across the United States took offense when Young Life released their Non-Negotiable document.[78] Christian Smith of the University of Notre Dame and Doug Campbell of Duke Divinity School wrote a response to the Young Life document titled "Why the New Young Life 'Non-Negotiable' Statement on Gospel Proclamation Needs to be Re-considered." Smith and Campbell concluded that Young Life was taking a stance through this point of "repent and then you shall be saved." They understood this to be conditional and sequential understanding of salvation that depended on human repentance and faith. This, in their view, was a type of "works righteousness" that does not reflect the sovereign love and grace of God.[79] They concluded that this was less a biblical position of salvation, and more a reflection of the American culture's "captivity to the rational choices of autonomous individuals to make contractual agreements as the basis of valid relationships."[80] They conclude that to make a suggestion that God had done nearly all the work of salvation *but* that teens need to fill in the last gap with their own confession and faith is "theologically misguided, organizationally parochial, and pastorally counter-productive in the subsequent discipleship of believing teens."[81]

This demand for "wholehearted commitment and mission unity" around the gospel proclamation document became visible when the Young Life organization fired eight of its staff people in the Raleigh/Durham area of North Carolina. Collin Hansen, a journalist with the *Christianity Today*, reported in February, 2008 that "Following a November statement outlining the "Non-Negotiables of Young Life's Gospel Proclamation, Young

77. McSwain, "Jesus in the Gospel," 4.

78. Tony Jones, a theologian known for his work in the emerging church culture, concluded that this stance in the proclamation document was "shortsighted and shallow in the are of sotierology." (www.tonyj.net)

79. Smith and Campbell, "Why the New Young Life," 1.

80. Ibid., 2.

81. Ibid. Italics in original.

Incarnational Theology: Christology, Soteriology, Campaigners

Life has fired or accepted resignations from all 10 staff members in the Durham-Chapel Hill area of North Carolina."[82] Campbell said McSwain and other YL area staff were resuming their efforts under the name Reality Ministries. He remains hopeful that the two sides can reconcile. "If Young Life held out its hand, we'd be only too happy to take it, because we all come from Young Life and that's what we know and care about," he said. "But that's in the hands of Young Life, really." Young Life's Swenson said the Non-Negotiables would serve as a reference point for staff members, ensuring consistency at YL clubs and camps. "There's a practical element to this that drives a lot of what we're attempting to do," he said.[83]

John Dart, of the journal *Christian Century* reported, "It appears, he said, that anyone who cannot completely endorse the eight-page statement on guidelines must leave the organization, and he cited the dismissals in North Carolina." New "nonnegotiable" guidelines for evangelism at Young Life ministries has led to the closing of a North Carolina office of the group and the claim by a national expert on youth and religion that the organization is moving in a fundamentalist and authoritarian direction.[84]

Jeff McSwain believed young people would sense a shift from the Trinitarian/incarnational model in contact work with the legal separation model presented to them during a week at Young Life camp.[85]

> In the last decade my mind has been changing about the best model of gospel proclamation within Young Life. Is it possible to change the model without losing the gospel itself? Yes, in fact, I would assert that this has already happened during the almost seventy year history of Young Life.... Is it possible that we could clearly and faithfully preach a Christ-centered gospel without the penal/legal formula and the bridge illustration paradigm? Yes. Is it possible that the legal separation model has actually obscured the Christ-centered nature of Young Life and the gospel? I believe so, and that is my purpose in writing this paper.[86]

Young Life claims to invite interpretation and flexibility within understanding in two ways: Rayburn claimed the best work of the organization was yet to be done, and the Young Life body claimed the pattern established by

82. Hansen, "Gospel Talk."
83. Ibid., 2.
84. Dart, "Young Life Draws Fire," 3.
85. McSwain, "Jesus Is the Gospel," 2.
86. Ibid.

Rayburn was one of tipping sacred cows. In the leadership training manual Young Life states, "Jim Rayburn used to say, 'The best Young Life work is yet to be done.' The giants of Young Life's past have written important chapters in our mission's history, but our call remains constant and current—the needs of kids today are more urgent than ever. As you begin your ministry with Young Life you become another chapter in our history. How would you like your chapter to read?"[87] In relationship to shaping Young Life club in a manner that would best suit the needs of young people in a specific area, they suggest answering questions of God and the community. "Have we [the Young Life community] come to a consensus that God is leading us in a different direction regarding club? If so, in what way are we going to verbally proclaim the Gospel?"[88] Young Life provides room for flexibility within the organization and seeks to understand how that would affect the proclamation of the gospel. However, as noted above, Young Life did not provide as much flexibility in the specific case of Jeff McSwain and his staff in North Carolina. Young Life concludes their section on tipping sacred cows by stating, "Jim Rayburn was an expert cow-tipper. He turned 'Christian camping' on its head and took the gospel outside the walls of church to kids on campus. Yet it has been rightly said that the best Young Life work is yet to be done. To move effectively forward in the future means asking hard questions, then doing what works and doing it well. And sometimes it might mean following in the founder's footsteps and tipping a sacred cow."[89]

The proclamation document closes with this statement:

> We affirm that it is both the responsibility and commitment of the senior leadership of Young Life to communicate these non-negotiables of proclamation and then to train our staff and volunteers on how to proclaim the Gospel.[90] Once our staff and volunteers are trained, we will hold them accountable for the content and clarity of our proclamation. We understand that there may be Young Life staff members or volunteers who would prefer to proclaim the Gospel another way. But because the issue of how we proclaim the Good News of Jesus Christ to kids is at the heart of what we do and because we are called to be stewards of this high and holy

---

87. Young Life, leadership training manual, 13.
88. Ibid., 132.
89. Ibid., 133.
90. In conversation with Ken Knipp, director of training for Young Life, they have introduced a new leadership training session for camp speakers in response to the Young Life proclamation document (14 May 2008, field journal).

responsibility, we will maintain our position as described in this paper. We must have wholehearted commitment and mission unity in the way we proclaim the Gospel of Jesus Christ.[91]

Leaders within the organization will now be held accountable for the manner in which they share the news of Jesus Christ, and are seeking for wholehearted commitment to that message. With these statements, Young Life seems to be attempting to create order out of a pattern of trial and error that was previously set.

So, although Young Life has set out doctrinal statements of faith that form a part of their ministry, it is actually the praxis that receives the emphasis. Because Jeff McSwain and others were not proclaiming the gospel in a manner in which the organization was comfortable, they were dismissed from the ministry of Young Life. I believe it was because of the loose nature of theological emphasis that Young Life was forced into articulating their non-negotiables when the practice of ministry in one area did not fit into what they believed was the Young Life way. Perhaps if their theological parameters had been established earlier in the life of the organization situations like the one documented would not have happened.

Conclusion

Though Young Life has a formal Statement of Faith and a new Non-Negotiable document that give structure to their ministry, they did not establish these tenets until much later in their organizational life as compared to Youth for Christ or InterVarsity Christian Fellowship. I argue that Young Life is more comfortable in their praxis of ministry rather than their theological articulation. Young Life establishes their doctrinal praxis and understanding on the methodological foundation of incarnational theology. As Young Life understands the role of relationships within their ministry so follows their understanding of theological positions of ministry. Christology, soteriology, discipleship and ecclesiology all follow a relational understanding of the faith. As Young Life articulates these beliefs in distinct ways, they articulate a distinct understanding of Christian doctrine to young people. In the following chapter I will show how Young Life, in similar means, articulates a unique message of Christianity that is nuanced to the culture of the organization. The chapter will show how Christianity is an attractive, strong and patriotic faith that you can experience at Young Life camp.

91. Young Life, "Non-Negotiables," 7.

4

Cultural Expression

IT WAS A PICTURE that caught my eye. I was looking through decades worth of *Young Life* magazines in the archives of the organization in Colorado Springs and the photograph grabbed my attention for some reason.

Cultural Expression

It was a black and white cover photo of a young man and a young woman canoeing together. For some reason this particular picture made me pause and wonder why this specific photograph was used for the edition of the magazine. But then, as my research continued, I came across three more photographs of a similar nature! Pictures of a young man and a young woman canoeing together on the cover of the magazine happened across three decades and it made me wonder, "What does this have to say about God? And what does this have to say about Young Life?" It was such a curiosity that it made an impression on my project and set the tone for the articulation of the *culture* of the Young Life organization.

The purpose of this project is to understand the various ways and manners in which the Young Life organization expresses their understanding of God. Because of the oral history tradition within the organization, it is also the purpose of this work to highlight the manner in which Young Life articulates their distinct Christian message to young people. In my previous chapter I highlighted the distinct doctrinal statements of Young Life and the manner in which they present their understanding of conservative evangelical theology through incarnational theology, Christology, soteriology, discipleship, and ecclesiology. Young Life, by presenting their theological position through these distinct statements, has shown themselves to be innovative in theological practice. In this chapter, however, I argue that Young Life presents a culturally nuanced message of Christianity through their organizational publications. I will articulate the cultural Christian message of Young Life as I discovered while working through archival material.

However, as I noted in the previous chapter, evangelical youth ministries such as Youth for Christ and InterVarsity Christian Fellowship adopted formal theological statements of faith at an early stage in their ministry. I also noted that the Young Life organization formalized statements of faith but at a much later date than their colleagues. This, I believe, has to do with the fact that Young Life operated from a methodological praxis of ministry as noted by historian Char Meredith as well as former Young Life staff person John Miller. Below I will highlight the methodology of ministry that shaped Young Life from the early stages of ministry.

Methodological Doctrine

Though looking at the statements of faith of Youth for Christ and InterVarsity Christian Fellowship in comparison to Young Life offers insights to the progression and emphasis of doctrinal stances, what is particularly interesting is the fact that Young Life established their methodological doctrine before any formal statements of faith. Young Life historians Char Meredith and John Miller both note the methodological position of Young Life was established early on in the ministry. Meredith notes that within ten years of organizational vitality, Young Life had guiding principles for their ministry. According to her, the principles that had survived the trial and error of the first decade came to be understood as common sense:

1. Go where kids congregate.
2. Accept them as they are.
3. Learn how to walk in wisdom to those outside the faith.
4. See the dignity of each unique person.
5. Find a neutral setting for the club meeting.
6. Create a climate that is informal.
7. Speak naturally in terms familiar to the vocabulary of the kids.
8. Communicate your certainties rather than flaunt your doubts.
9. Consider it a sin to bore kids, especially with the gospel.
10. Build on their instinct for adventure.
11. Capitalize on the elements of good humor and music to establish an openness to the gospel.[1]

And in similar fashion, four statements of praxis molded the understanding and ministry of John Miller who began his tenure with the organization in 1946. Miller began new Young Life clubs in Washington D.C.; Denver, Colorado; Leland, Mississippi; and Fresno, California. He also was head of Trail West Lodge in Colorado for ten years and during his later years with the organization provided leadership for fundraising banquets. Miller retired in 1982 but wrote a book for Young Life in 1991 that set forth his understanding of the organizational model of ministry:

---

1. Meredith, *It's a Sin to Bore a Kid*, 53.

Cultural Expression

1. Walk in wisdom toward them that are without.
2. It's a sin to bore a kid with the gospel.
3. Win the right to be heard.
4. Assume our young audience does not know anything about the Christian faith. Therefore, always be in the posture of a teacher—never a preacher. There is tremendous difference.[2]

Miller contends the four tenets above were received as he participated in a leadership seminar with Jim Rayburn in 1946. Miller believed that the ministry should return to these roots as they contemplate how to make the ministry most effective.

As we can see, the methodological practice of Young Life was understood at an early stage within the ministry. John Miller believes he received words of practical wisdom that marked his ministerial practice in 1946. I believe that, although Young Life has formal statements of faith documented, Young Life has much earlier statements of Christianity that have given structure to their Christian message. I also contend that, as the methodology of Young Life was established in the early days, so too was their Christian message as presented in various publications of the ministry.

The *Young Life* magazine,[3] first published in March 1944, was a monthly magazine directed towards high school students and sold by subscription. The March 1954 issue gives a small insight to the measure of the magazine. Describing an increase in magazine circulation by 50% from the previous two years, the circulation was reaching 13,000 young people in the US, as well as twenty-three foreign countries.[4] The YLM of 1975 states the purpose of the publication for that era: "Here is your all new read-it-and-stretch *Young Life* magazine. Sized to fit in your jeans—no hands necessary. Aimed to give you a 'club in covers' to go home with . . . to take you from where you are to where you gotta stretch to get. Read it and laugh, read it and weep, read it and sing, but read it!"[5] After 1960 the YLM changed in format and frequency. Over the years the name of the Young Life publication has varied from "Young Life" to "Focus on Youth" to "Relationships."[6] There have been other publications produced by Young

---

2. Miller, *Back to the Basics*, 49.
3. I will refer to the *Young Life* magazine as YLM from here on for efficiency.
4. *Young Life* magazine, March 1954, 15.
5. Young Life, *Focus on Youth*, Spring 1975, 2.
6. *Relationships* has remained the name of the publication consistently since the

103

Life to supplement the ministry, namely the "Focus on Youth" publication that was intended for adults for the purpose of highlighting issues within the adolescent world. The purpose of this chapter is to follow main themes that are highlighted by Young Life through these various publications as they appear over the decades of the organization. I argue that although the vehicle of communication may vary for Young Life, the distinct Christian message of the organization remains the same.

My research has uncovered four themes in the *YLM* and other official publications: Christianity is attractive, Christianity is "not for sissies" (the message of sports), being a good Christian is being a good American (the message of military and nationality), and experiencing the best week of your life (the story of Young Life camp). The magazine takes us right into the heart of the historic and foundational cultural messages of Young Life. We will begin by looking at the message of the attractiveness of Christianity and the foundation of the good-looking Jesus.

Young Life's Jesus: Making Christianity Attractive

From the beginning, the words "making Christianity attractive" would form an important backdrop for the work and words of Young Life. Through articles and photographs, it is clear that *YLM* editors intended to portray a Christianity that is desirable. In the first *YLM* printed in February 1944, Jim Rayburn, the founder of Young Life, sets the tone for the attractiveness of Christ. "Yes sir! Jesus Christ is LIFE! Jesus Christ is really attractive! So, we seek to present Him in the most attractive way."[7] Rayburn goes on to state that the Young Life Campaign is in the business of presenting the Lord Jesus Christ to the high school "gang" because they believe he is the most fascinating person in the universe. The goal of the *YLM* was to present something the high school "gang" would really like. The stated belief was that Jesus would completely captivate the heart of any young person who knows him, and the success of the magazine came because Jesus was the only one full of abundant life.[8] The attractiveness of Christ is also stated directly in May of 1951 and October of 1956.

1980s. This is the current form of the Young Life publication and is intended for a wider audience than the first *Young Life* magazine of 1944. *Relationships* is sent out to all those interested in Young Life: students, staff, volunteers and donors (free of charge).

7. *Young Life* magazine, February 1944, 2.
8. *Young Life* magazine, March 1945.

The *YLM* believed Jesus Christ was everything a young person wanted, if they just knew it. "[Jesus is] the most wonderful, the most attractive, the strongest, most gracious, loving person this world has ever seen."[9] The desire was for every high school kid in the country to know Jesus, and it was up to those in Young Life to show kids what they were missing. The belief was that young people would want Jesus if they knew who he was.[10]

Rayburn states in May 1948 that Christianity is the most attractive proposition for a young person because Young Life leaders are "100% attractive in every way!" (He states that Jesus Christ is the most attractive person Young Life leaders know). His attractiveness message continues, "Everything about Him is tops. Ah yes, everything that is manly and loveable and attractive, is all combined in the Lord Jesus Christ—and only in Him."[11] Rayburn goes on to say in June of 1948 that everything Jesus offers is attractive, and the hope of a Christian is different. As a Christian becomes older, hope becomes brighter—life becomes one that "really clicks." He states that life gets better forever after someone becomes a Christian and that is one of the benefits of receiving Christ. This better life proposition, this message of Jesus Christ, is the most attractive message in the world according to Young Life. Jesus is attractive, his plan of salvation is attractive, and the life of the individual who "gets squared away with Him, is terrifically attractive" even to those who have not thought about God.[12]

In addition to the pervasive presence of the attractiveness of Christ himself, a similar message of the attractiveness of Christianity is displayed through the magazine's photographs. My research of the history of Young Life began in the summer of 2005 in the archives of the Young Life headquarters in Colorado Springs, Colorado. Initial research of the *YLM* suggested an interesting pattern—photographs of couples in canoes. I first

9. *Young Life* magazine, November 1953, 4.

10. Ibid. Philip J. Lee, in *Against the Protestant Gnostics*, has this to say about knowing Christ: "The American evangelical tradition has seemed to feel that orthodoxy could be assured by keeping Jesus Christ at the center of its faith. In the hymns, Scripture selection, preaching and prayers of evangelicals, Jesus is certainly given center stage. The center-stage Jesus, however, has been given a very limited role. He is not responsible for the Creation. He is not the Incarnate God who, thereby, has access to all persons alike: Muslims, Jews, atheists, Hindus, as well as Christians. He is not empowered to bring healing to the world apart from the conversion of individuals. The Jesus of this mind-set must be *known* in order to effect change; his only function is to bring saving knowledge." (Lee, *Against the Protestant Gnostics*, 107)

11. *Young Life* magazine, May 1948, 2.

12. *Young Life* magazine, June 1952, 3.

began to sense a theme of the attractiveness of Christianity after I viewed those photographs of couples in a canoe.[13] After finding a number of these photographs in the *YLM*, questions were raised: What was the purpose in using a photograph of that nature? What does it say about Young Life's belief in God?[14] If Young Life is about making Christianity attractive, as they state through their words, are they also making a similar statement through the photographs they used?[15]

In the one hundred and eighty eight magazines reviewed for the years 1944-1960, thirty-three had a photograph of a couple on the cover (17%). Criterion for a couple was one young man and one young woman on the cover by themselves. The activities these young people were engaged in ranged from bicycling[16] to hiking[17] to gazing into each-others eyes.[18] The February 1945 cover shows a young woman sitting on a set of bleachers while a young man ties her ice skates. The January 1958 issue shows a young man helping a young woman up after she has fallen while skiing.

If everything that is "manly and loveable and attractive" is found in Jesus Christ[19] perhaps that can be viewed through the photographs of couples used. But attractiveness was not limited to photographs of couples.[20]

---

13. Field Journal, 2005.

14. Ibid.

15. A photograph of a couple in a canoe happened once a decade—June 1945, October 1959, August 1960, and Fall 1972. The June 1945 photograph shows a young man paddling the canoe, his back to the camera, while the young woman sits facing him.

16. *Young Life* magazine, June 1946.

17. *Young Life* magazine, September 1945.

18. *Young Life* magazine: September 1944, March 1946, October 1946, February 1948, June 1949, November 1951.

19. *Young Life* magazine, May 1948, 2.

20. The message of the attractiveness of Christ did not always hit the mark. Margaret Campbell from Washington State College in the December 1944 in her letter to the editor stated, "Dear Campaigners, I am one of those 'Sunnysiders' who has gone to college, and like all good co-eds I have been looking for some pin-ups for my room. I had seen every type, I believe, from Varga Girl to B-19, but today I found the ideal pin-up for my room—my October issue of Young Life came, and after I had read it cover to cover I decided that there could be nothing better. Now several hours after putting them up—I am pleased as punch!" (*Young Life* magazine, December 1944, 2.)

CULTURAL EXPRESSION

The cover photograph of the August 1946 issue shows a young man who is wet wearing a bathing suit ready to dive into the water. The issue includes a fictional piece about a lifeguard on duty.[21] The July 1948 issue shows a young man in a bathing suit and sunglasses stretched out by the water on a beach.

The issue includes a fictional piece about a young man named Bob Bronson who was daydreaming on the beach.[22] The June 1950 cover shows a young woman smiling up away from the camera wearing a crown. The inside cover stated she was the winner of the Miss City Beautiful contest in Memphis, Tennessee, and "she'll be at Star Ranch this summer boys."[23] The December 1953 cover photograph is of a young man skiing. The photograph shows him standing with his poles and skis draped over his shoulder—sunglasses on looking off into the distance.

21. *Young Life* magazine, August 1946, 14.
22. *Young Life* magazine, July 1948, 14.
23. *Young Life* magazine, June 1950, 3.

Finally, the March issue of 1955 has a cover photograph of two young women sitting outside and eating dessert. The editor states, "Since our magazine leans heavily towards the fellow's viewpoint this month, we thought we'd let the girls have the cover . . . Martha and Beryl are 'having their cake and eating it 'just prior to the chili lunch for the whole [Campaigners] crowd.'"[24]

Continuing the words of Jim Rayburn and the staff of Young Life with photographs used within the magazine, the attractiveness of the Christian faith became the foundational message of the organization. In an attempt to convince young people that Jesus Christ is really attractive, Young Life presents them with words and photographs of people who are visually attractive. Has this affected the organization to attract only the "cool" kids? Is the culture of Young Life one that attracts the good looking people? The historical narrative as found in the textual record reveals a theme of the attractiveness of Christ.

24. *Young Life* magazine, March 1955, 3.

CULTURAL EXPRESSION

This theme of the attractiveness of Christ becomes the connecting tissue that holds other themes together throughout the *YLM*. Themes of sporting life, military and political life, and the camping ethos of the organization seem to build upon the theme of attractiveness throughout. Christianity enables one to succeed in sports and grow in strength while serving the military. Further Christianity can be experienced in an enticing way at Young Life camp while swimming, horseback riding, or listening to entertaining people. And, as they share the message of Christ with young people, Young Life utilizes language that will enable them to articulate the message in an attractive way.

Making the Message Attractive through Articulation[25]

Jim Rayburn believed that other Christian leaders were missing the mark in presenting the gospel of Christ in ways young people would enjoy. He stated, "I believe the indifference of young people to things Christian could be quickly corrected by the right kind of leadership—a leadership that would drive right to the heart of the Christian faith and make it simple and clear is what is needed."[26] Rayburn's casual language and simple message was attractive to young people in the early days of the ministry.

This message of clarity and simplicity in communication of the gospel is described in the January 1969 issue of the *YLM*. They believe the clearest way to communicate the gospel is through the "person-to-person" encounter. They believe the communication of the gospel must be combined with the "human warmth of a life touching a life." They go on to say, "The right words alone will not do it; the neat familiar phrases may even kill it. In relationship *love is felt*. There is no pat answer. Communication of more than superficial quality is a complicated process. Communication of the superb message of God calls for nothing less than our lives—available and vulnerable."[27] Here Young Life is making a case for a relationship-based model of communication—a style of presentation that values the person, not the precise construction of the message.

Later in 1969, Young Life articulated succinctly their understanding of communicating the gospel with young people in their leadership-training manual. They state, "God desires to communicate His message through us to the teenage crowd in language they will understand. We need to be skilled communicators of the message: This means knowing and understanding our Message, understanding the communication process, and presenting the message in a dynamic, winsome manner."[28]

This style-over-substance emphasis is clearly expressed in an interview with volunteer leaders Andy and Marian Nyboer[29] in an article titled

---

25. In the history chapter I discussed the effort Jim Rayburn made to connect to the emerging youth culture through the casual language he used.

26. *Young Life* magazine, April 1948, 4.

27. *Young Life* magazine, January 1969, 2.

28. Young Life, leadership training manual, 6.

29. Young Life, *Focus on Youth*, Winter 1975, 8–11. In this article, Andy and Marian Nyboer discuss their oldest daughter Jackie who was drawn to Young Life in high school, leading the entire family into Young Life. Jackie (Nyboer) VanWieren has lived in

"We Live Two Full Lives" in the Winter 1975 issue. In explaining the draw of the Nyboer family to the ministry of Young Life, Andy describes it like this: "We found that the questions that our own children had were not being adequately answered. When we were exposed to the Young Life projection of basic Christianity, we all liked it. They were using a language Marian and I could more easily understand; and our children were understanding it for the first time!" Andy goes on to articulate the importance of communication within Young Life. "Communication, I guess, is the name of the game,' Andy was wrestling with the basics that really count with kids. "I guess to talk their language without using the same words they use is part of whole thing. I know if you try to use their words, the first thing they do is laugh at you and mimic—ridicule really! They'll spot somebody who isn't sincere. What they want is for you to be really you–really genuinely you!"[30] The Young Life language became an entry point not only for the children of Andy and Marian Nyboer, but an entry point for them as adults as well. With this grasp of basic Christianity, the Nyboer's became Young Life leaders in their area. It was a message "we all liked." Andy came to recognize the importance of "talk[ing] their language" as a Young Life leader. Communication of the Christian message, in the vernacular language of young people of the time, is "the name of the game."

From issues of the *YLM* from the 1970s[31] I noticed that club talks from Young Life camp were presented in their entirety. What became clear to me was the casual language utilized in the presentation of the gospel message within these documents. We begin with an article from the October 1967 issue of the *YLM*. In this presentation of a Young Life club talk titled "Prodigal Son—A Young Life Club Talk" we are given a "favorite story in the New Testament:"

> It was great at first. He took the money and went into town and bought new clothes, and found him a girl, and got high. "Man! I've rebelled. Here I am going someplace. I'm free." He lived it up there, and then moved on until he was a long ways from home. He'd blown all his money. Food was hard to hustle. He had to get a job. And before he knew it he was slopping pigs, and eating the stuff the pigs were eating. At this point Christ tells us, "he comes to his senses." He wakes up. "What the heck? I had it made back

---

Holland, Michigan, for over thirty years and has contributed to the work of Young Life in this community.

30. Ibid.

31. During the presidency of Bill Starr the magazine was named *Focus on Youth*.

home. I had everything I needed and more. Where's the freedom? What is freedom?" The big thing is you have to see where you are. And you have to be willing to say you're sorry. This is what confession is—saying "I'm sorry" to God. Then you find a Father who loves you waiting there. The same kind of father the kid found in California. After you've admitted your guilt, your loneliness, you take your face out of your hands, and look up. In place of shame comes exuberance . . . We see God crying out, "I love you. I do care. But I'm not going to force you to love Me. I'm here. If you want Me, get off that train, get out of that pig pen, and come home. I've given you my Son that you might have life, that you might be really free." The way home is Christ. The way to freedom is obedience to the Father.[32]

In an article titled "The Conforming Son—A Young Life Club Talk" from the January 1968 issue, readers are met once again with a story of the Prodigal Son, but this time with a focus on the older brother. You read phrases like "once I had a fella in club," "could have gotten him into big trouble with the fuzz," and "he didn't leave the old man." The connection is made between a Young Life kid who stole beer from a beer truck every week in high school with the older brother of the story who remained behind after the prodigal son left. "Course most of you wouldn't fool around like that. Most of you are too proper to go against the wishes of your parents. Maybe the fear of getting caught is what really holds you from being more gross than you are. You know, in all love and honesty, my friends, the majority of you remind me—not of the Prodigal, but of the older son in the Bible story . . . Christ is the open door into the Father's house as much for the one who carries out his duties, as for the one who runs away."[33] This club talk, given at a Young Life camp, couches the story of the Prodigal Son in the vernacular language of the day. Using words like "fuzz" (for police), "fella" and "old man," the message of life with God is presented both for those who rebel as well as for those who remain behind. These messages of the late 1960s depict Young Life as speaking the language of the time.

The Spring 1990 issue provides an interview with long-time Young Life leader Anne Cheairs who was asked to share her memories of Young Life club in the early days of the organization. Having been asked and given memories of such things like the original format of a Young Life club, Jim Rayburn's philosophy, strongest memories of club, and the role of prayer

32. *Young Life* magazine, October 1967, 13.
33. *Young Life* magazine, January 1968, "The Conforming Son," 13.

in club work, the last question and answer of the article changes the focus by asking her to challenge today's Young Life club and leaders: "*What is your challenge to today's Young Life club leaders?* I would remind them that the message is the focus. It is the jewel in the ring. Work to make every club every week a great club. Remember Jim's statement, 'It is the continual hearing of the gospel that will win a person to Christ.' I wonder if there's too much dependence on camps, as wonderful as they are, instead of bringing kids to respond after a strong year of clubs."[34] Cheairs believes the message is the focus for Young Life, the "jewel in the ring" of the ministry.

Interim president Ted Johnson, in relating his first-time experience with Young Life, described the high-spirited fun and resort atmosphere at camp. He goes on to pinpoint that what attracted him was the proclamation of the gospel. "But what attracted us most was Young Life's PROCLAMATION of Jesus Christ. This was unique! Young Life leaders just know how to talk about Jesus. Call it style. It's sensitive and informal and friendly. They communicate in a conversational way in terms that kids can understand and appreciate. A teenager at a recent Young Life banquet reported, 'I like my leader. He talks to us about God like he isn't paid to do it!' That says it."[35] With this short statement from the interim president, Johnson easily sums up what had been attracting leaders and students alike for decades within Young Life. This conversational style of communicating the gospel in the organization became a featured emphasis within the *YLM*. Through articles and editorials, Young Life repeats over and over again the style of communication that drew so many young people to the organization.

Young Life laid a foundation of utilizing a casual style of proclamation that would make the message of Jesus attractive. Establishing an emphasis on a casual style of gospel proclamation, Young Life worked to establish their message based on the vernacular of young people of the time. Whether couching the message of the Prodigal Son in terms like "getting in trouble with the fuzz" or "he didn't leave the old man," the sensitive, informal and friendly message that people seem to enjoy communicates Christianity in ways young people (as well as adults) will be attracted to. Anne Cheairs reminded the organization that Jim Rayburn emphasized the message during his tenure—that it was the jewel in the ring of Young Life.[36]

---

34. *Relationships*, Spring 1990, back page.
35. *Relationships*, Spring 1993, 3–4. Capitalization in original.
36. *Relationships*, Spring 1990.

However, attractiveness through the articulation of the Christian message was not the only method Young Life employed to reach young people. They also emphasized the value and the role of humor in their ministry.

Attractiveness of Christianity through Humor

The organization stresses that one part of the ministry through Young Life club came straight from Jim Rayburn: the importance of good humor. Training materials state, "Humor changes over time, but from the very beginning, Young Life meetings have always had a healthy dose of laughter and fun in them."[37] Young Life further establishes their incarnational theology on the understanding that humor is one of the best ways to establish relationships. "We use humor a lot in Young Life. It may well be one of our best tools in establishing relationships with kids. Jesus Christ said, 'I have come that they may have life, and have it to the full,' John 10:10. Laughter and fun are one link in the chain of a full life. Bob Mitchell, former president of Young Life, said it best: 'Embrace kids with humor.' What a wonderful privilege."[38] This abundant life that Christ offers is a clear statement Jim Rayburn repeated often in his days of work with Young Life.

The son of founder Jim Rayburn, Rayburn III, documents the opinion of Young Life staff members and the impression they received through the humor of the founder himself:

> Jim helped us to see that Jesus laughed, and that he still laughs, that Christ is also King in the realm of humor. And in our hearts we felt relieved; God seemed closer. Laughing together became a part of worship. Jim showed us Christ's compassion for the little people: the losers, the drunks, the prisoners, the liars, the cheaters, the weary, and the heavy-laden. And in our hearts we liked that too, for it made us feel that God still cares for such as we. Jim taught us that we can learn as much about God in climbing a mountain as we're likely to in an hour of church. And in our hearts, we felt lighter; we've all been bored in the sanctuary, but days in the high country are remembered. Jim gave us purpose, and a dream. And in our hearts, we soared, for we had a reason for our being. We felt we counted somehow, and that felt good. Someone loved and wanted us; his name is Jesus.[39]

37. Young Life, leadership training manual, 83.
38. Ibid., 121.
39. Rayburn III, *Dance, Children, Dance*, 207.

Cultural Expression

Rick Yates, author of *Skits for Camp and Club*, a manual for Young Life staff, outlines the connection between incarnational and relational theology with humor and fun. This manual, produced by the resources department of Young Life, was distributed as material that could be used specifically for Young Life club and/or ministry everywhere. Yates explains the resource manual for skits in this manner: "Young Life's ministry has been, is and always will be, outreach evangelism to disinterested adolescents. We share the gospel of Jesus Christ with those kids who have not yet committed their lives to Him. Our incarnational, relational style of evangelization requires significant time of contact work between leaders and kids. Laughter and discussion are clear elements of outreach evangelism."[40] Yates believes that in the early days of Young Life the organization became known for its fun and good humor. "Adventure, laughter and humor were trademarks and very appealing to disinterested kids. Clubs and camps always had fun times as important elements. Young Life people were fun-loving and attractive. Humor, laughter, fun and attractiveness are still important to us. Kids who are bored or turned-off to Christian words or actions are usually drawn to fun activities and fun-loving people."[41] Yates' own experience as a student in Young Life shaped his Christian commitment through humor and fun.

"Humor was the great common denominator in Young Life. Kids from all kinds of backgrounds and situations would get together, and laughter would unite them. I don't think it was a manipulative device but rather an outgrowth of having 'life more abundant.'"[42] Yates' earliest memories while in high school always included laughter. He speculated that kids have come to know the Lord through Young Life because they were first attracted to Christ through having fun. "I'm sure that there are many who have made a commitment to Christ years after their Young Life experience because they remember having fun at a Christian meeting. I know that I wouldn't have gone back to Young Life if I hadn't been having fun. It is still true today that high school kids want to have fun. Humor is a big part of life."[43] Yates concludes that humor in Young Life came with Jim Rayburn. He believed Rayburn was funny and that he was able to tell stories with humor that allowed the Bible to come alive for young people.[44]

---

40. Yates, *Skits for Camp*, 2.
41. Ibid.
42. Ibid., 4.
43. Ibid.
44. Ibid., 3.

Current president of Young Life Denny Rydberg[45] was also committed to establishing his emphasis on humor in the first article that introduced him as president in a 1993 article in the *YLM*. Rydberg himself underscores his sense of humor in his description: "How does the new president of Young Life describe himself? 'I'm a person with a sense of humor. I love to laugh. I love it at night when the whole family can be at home and we're not doing anything. I have a deep sense of loyalty to friends. I have a deep love for Jesus Christ; I want to do what He wants me to do . . . '"[46] Humor and laughter are the first descriptors of the current president—establishing his credibility within an organization that believes young people are attracted to Christ through the avenue of humor.

Young Life, from the foundation of Jim Rayburn and his persona, has made Christianity attractive through the foundation of good humor and fun. Rayburn believed it was a "sin to bore kids" and would go to great lengths to engage young people through his sense of humor. Embracing humor in an effort to utilize laughter as an outreach of evangelism is a way in which Young Life makes Christianity attractive for young people.[47] Rick Yates expands on the idea of leadership within Young Life. "I do believe one of the important jobs of a leader is to find the funny people around him or her and utilize their gifts of humor. We need to recruit funny people and get them in front of kids."[48] With the use of humor, Young Life believes leaders can add a link in the chain for a life full of Christ. The use of humor, then, makes the Christian message appealing for students who may be disinterested in Jesus.

45. Young Life went to great lengths to highlight the various ministries Rydberg had been a part of previous to his appointment as president. Note that *The Wittenberg Door* was started as an underground satirical magazine for Christians. "Denny comes to the mission having spent most of his life in Christian ministry. He served as Director of University Ministries at University Presbyterian Church in Seattle. He was pivotal in distributing the Warner Brothers *Jesus* film. He was a co-owner of Youth Specialties, providing youth workers with materials and creative ideas so they could reach kids more effectively for Christ. He also edited the Christian humor magazine, "The Wittenberg Door" in the 1970s. So he brings to Young Life a wealth of past experiences and a continued commitment to serve Jesus Christ" (*Relationships*, Fall 1993, 11–14).

46. *Relationships*, Fall 1993, 11–14.

47. This language is also used in the October 1953 issue of the *Young Life* magazine. Rayburn states that friendliness is the "major" in Young Life. "There is a quality of friendliness and love that the Lord Jesus will put in our lives if we will stay close to Him. And without it His work becomes fruitless and barren. Friendliness is our major in Young Life" (*Young Life* magazine, October 1953, 4).

48. Yates, *Skits for Camp*, 4.

Cultural Expression

In this section I have presented the manner in which Young Life makes Christianity attractive for young people: through photographs and words, through an attractive message of Christ that utilizes the casual language of young people, and the use of humor that attracts young people to the person of Christ through laughter. In the next section I will present the cultural Christian message of strength and sports in the Young Life organization.

Christianity According to Young Life: "Not for Sissies"

The second major theme that emerges from the data, "Christianity is not for sissies," comes from the arena of sports. Of the one hundred and eighty-eight magazines reviewed from 1944 to 1960, forty-one had photographs of young people participating in sporting activities (23%). The method of criteria I adopted was that of observing scenes where young people were clothed in school sports uniforms. It did not include photographs of people riding horses or driving racecars, for instance. The very first issue of the magazine (March 1944) has a cover photograph of a young man playing basketball. Again, the magazine utilized written words with photographs to display the theme of sports and the message of "Christianity is not for sissies."[49]

The emphasis on sports ranges from articles on teams and the individuals on those teams to sport stars of the day. The interaction between athletics and the Young Life ministry was intertwined in a variety of ways. The January 1957 issue deepens that connection on the club level and the message from a grassroots leader emerges. The article, taken from the Riverside, California, newspaper focuses on the undefeated season of the football team and the rise of Young Life club in the school. Interviewing club leader Donald Taylor, author Joe Wimer states that as Poly High's athletic fortunes have improved, Young Life club has gone from fifteen to one

---

49. One explicit use of this term was used not by a sports athlete, but by cowboy Roy Rogers in a January 1955 article. In the article titled "King and Queen of the West" Dale Evans and Roy Rogers give their testimony of faith and their source of happiness from the world of cowboys. Roy Rogers states, "I've been getting a lot of mail from kids—boys especially—who ask me if I don't think it's pretty sissy for them to go to Sunday school. I want to say right here and now that it isn't sissy at all. In fact, I think it's one of the best things any kid can do . . . Now this was quite a statement for a cowboy to come out with, right in the middle of a rootin', tootin', arena show" (*Young Life* magazine, January 1955, 6 & 11).

hundred students. The article concludes with the statement that students have gained an awareness of spiritual values through Young Life that they have then applied in athletics and life. "Christianity needn't be only for sissies, Taylor says. And his membership roster proves the point. Some pretty rugged boys are included."[50]

A similar theme of the interaction between sports and the spiritual life is found in the July 1954 issue as well. The article, featuring the sport of lacrosse on the eastern seaboard of the United States, gives the basics of the sport as well as an interview with the Young Life leader Bob Kirkley who also assists with coaching. Kirkley advocates that sports participation conditions the Young Lifer physically, and Young Life aids in the development of the spiritual life of the individual. The article states, "Lacrosse and Young Life have learned to work together hand in hand."[51]

High school students themselves also wrote articles on sports. In an article titled "God Scored Our Touchdowns," (September 1952) student Rusty Gunn discusses the combination of prayer and football. Gunn, a player on the Arlington, Texas, high school team, in an attempt to bring God into the lives of others, suggests to the captain of the football team that they pray before every game. Upon including prayer as part of the season, they found themselves undefeated at the end of the year. Gunn comes to three conclusions about prayer and football: he decides never to pray for victory but to pray for power and strength, he prays nothing would be held against opponents, and he never pressures teammates about religious beliefs but does invite them to church. He states, "Football is a fine place to introduce a person to prayer . . . You might think that God has no place in a rough, tough game like football. I say God has a place anywhere. You might argue that prayer cannot help you do something like winning a football game. I don't think you could convince me or my team of that, because, you see, we won the State Championship for one reason: God scored our touchdowns."[52]

Dick Frey, a college football player at Texas A&M, wrote an article about the combination of Christianity, football, and happiness. He states that it is impossible to be unhappy when you let Christ have his way and walk step by step with him. Christianity makes the happy-go-lucky life an easy one to lead. Frey goes on to compare the Christian life with that of a football player. "I like to compare this part of Christian living with that

50. *Young Life* magazine, January 1957, 11.
51. Ibid., 21.
52. Gunn, "God Scored," 7-8.

of a football player. Every football player I have ever seen gets knocked down many times. Even all-Americans get knocked around lots of times in a single ball game. The thing that makes them great is that they don't stay down. They bounce right back up and get into play again. The only difference between that and the Christian life is that Christ is there to pull us up if we'll just let him."[53]

The emphasis on sports is further illustrated through featured stories about celebrity athletes. The first famous sports figure to be given attention was Gil Dodds,[54] the first American to break the four-minute mile. He first appeared on the back cover of the May 1944 issue. Dodds states that great athletes—the champions—are ones who center their lives on Christ. His hardest opponents in running have been those who look to God. He notes that Christ is always near, and nearer when Dodds needs him most.

In the second piece written on Dodds for the January 1945 issue, Dodds' life history is the focus of the article. In it, Dodds mentions that running is just a hobby for him but his real job in life is serving Jesus Christ. He believes the only way he broke the record was through prayer. Dodds says specifically to *YLM* readers, "Now is the time to make your life decision and I trust it is for Christ. He has everything to offer. The world may ridicule you and call you a 'Holy Joe,' but I have found the world really respects you if you stand out and out for what you believe."[55]

In the March 1945 issue, Dodds is linked to the positive endorsement of Sunday School stating, "You'd hardly call a long distance running champ a sissy, would you?" The article, "You Think Sunday School is Sissy," continues with the message of the ruggedness of Christ. "Do you know that Christ has no use for sissies? It's a fact! Look at the original twelve disciples. Don't see any sissies among them, do you? The Lord called out fishermen, farmers, laborers to follow Him—real he-men with callouses on their hands and muscles on their bodies."[56] The article goes on to state that the Lord is looking for similar young people today—those that are courageous and not afraid of the sneers of the gang. The issue continues to report that Dodds,

53. *Young Life* magazine, October 1951, 16.

54. Gil Dodds became a popular spokesperson for evangelistic youth ministries of the 1940s and 1950s. He not only toured with Rayburn and the Young Life organization, but also gave his message of Christ with the Youth for Christ movement. He often connected his world record in the mile with his faith in Christ (Meredith, *It's a Sin to Bore a Kid*; Larson, *Youth for Christ*).

55. *Young Life* magazine, January 1945, 10.

56. Ibid., 13.

in conjunction with Jim Rayburn and Young Life, visited Young Life clubs in six states, covering fifty meetings in fifteen different cities. Dodds gave exhibition races, interviews, and posed for photographs.[57] Dodds, "a champion miler and Young Life friend," presented Cleburne Price with the first Young Life Top Athlete Award in January of 1951.[58]

University of California Los Angeles (UCLA) football star Don Moomaw, first featured in an article in May 1952, became a nation wide name and a Christian, as well. Through a relationship with Bill Bright, founder of Campus Crusade for Christ, Moomaw began exploring the Christian faith. His conversion experience came in a football game against school rival University of Southern California (USC). Moomaw recalls, "That Saturday we were playing SC. During the game I was praying hard. About midway through the third quarter, I don't know why, I was everywhere the ball was. I intercepted it and stepped over into the end zone. My heart was just crying. I was happy because I knew for the first time there was a power beyond myself."[59] Through prayer, the article says, Moomaw was able to make a touchdown and salvage the season.

The combination of prayer and football continued for Moomaw. In the September 1953 issue, Moomaw writes of his experience playing in the North-South all-star game. Having not played well in the first half, Moomaw decided to spend some time in prayer during halftime. Upon entering the locker room, Moomaw slipped into a shower stall and thought, "I need to get with my Coach and Quarterback, Jesus Christ." Having spent a few moments in prayer, Moomaw went on to recover a fumble for a touchdown in the second half. "It makes a difference to play the game with Jesus Christ as your Quarterback!" he states. "Now I can honestly say that any touchdown I have scored, or any All-American team I have played on, cannot compare with the thrill I have received in knowing Christ as my Savior. Everyone is either playing for Him or against Him. What team are you on?"[60]

In an article featuring Steve Largent, a professional football player in the National Football League[61] (NFL) for the Seattle Seahawks, Largent gave

57. *Young Life* magazine, March 1945, 18.
58. *Young Life* magazine, January 1951, 10–11.
59. *Young Life* magazine, May 1952, 10.
60. *Young Life* magazine, September 1953, 6–7.
61. Joe Gibbs, a former coach in the National Football League, was also connected to Young Life and worked on behalf of the organization to attract interest in the ministry. Gibbs "of NFL and NASCAR fame is to plan an area interest meeting for Young Life. The meeting is going to be held in Gibbs' large auditorium sometime this spring. King

praise to Young Life for both the level of energy as well as being relationship oriented. Having begun his relationship with the Young Life organization, Largent went to his first Young Life club not to hear the message, but to make a scene with other football players from his team. "Initially I went because my friends went. Like most high school sophomores, I was looking for something to do to get out of the house. After going to club a few times, I grew attracted to the energy, the activities and the leaders of Young Life, so I kept going back."[62] Largent had a well-rounded experience of Young Life, he went on to become a student leader in college and later acted as a spokesman as a professional athlete. Largent concludes, "I think back on the Jim Rayburn quote: 'It's a sin to bore a kid with the gospel.' Young Life has done anything but that. It has always been a relationship-oriented ministry that has continued to share the gospel in a very effective way.' In the game of life, you can almost hear the announcer yell, 'Touchdown, Young Life!'"[63]

Brady Quinn, college quarterback for Notre Dame, was featured in an article titled "Going Long" in the Winter 2004 issue of the *YLM*. Quinn, who played professional football for numerous teams and is now a commentator for television, was part of a Young Life Campaigner Bible study group called the "James Gang" because of their study of the book of James every Friday morning in the local donut shop. Young Life leader Rob 'Crock' Crocker describes the hopes of some in Young Life: "Of course, when kids leave Young Life for college we hope some will become Young Life leaders. And many do. But all of them have a ministry. That's what we're preparing them for. Brady's ministry is football"[64] And Quinn expresses what is important to him in his relationship with his former Young Life leader, "I have a really close relationship to Crock. I can talk to him about anything—school, sports, my girlfriend and my faith. He gives me great advice. It might sound funny with our age difference and all, but Crock's one of the best friends I've ever had."[65] Though some Young Life students become leaders as they transition to their college years, some have the "ministry of football." Football then becomes the cultural vehicle for the message of Christianity and football players the messengers.

Solomon types take note. Sounds like a good place for an excellent find" (*Relationships*, Spring/Summer 1999, 11).

62. *Relationships*, Fall 1995, 26.
63. *Relationships*, Fall 1995, 25–27.
64. *Relationships*, Winter 2004, 8.
65. Ibid.

But the impact of sports is not relegated to football alone. Those in professional baseball and basketball have also had an impact in areas of Young Life, as illustrated in articles from Fall and Winter 2005. "Going to Bat for Kids" described the faith of professional baseball player Eric Chavez. Having been moved by the terrorist attacks of September 2001, Chavez gave his life to Christ and wanted an avenue in which to share his faith and be a blessing to others. Through connections with the chaplain of the Oakland A's, Chavez was introduced to Young Life and was immediately won over. For every home run hit, Chavez donated money for kids to attend Young Life camp. The article concludes, "Hope is not what the terrorists wanted to give Americans. They plotted fear, death and destruction, but up from the ashes rose an All-American baseball player, swinging for more than just the fences–batting kids home to Jesus Christ."[66]

The Fall 2005 issue of the *YLM* describes Woodland, California, Young Life club. Bobby Jackson, a basketball player with the Sacramento Kings of the National Basketball Association, accompanied the team chaplain to Young Life club. The report stated, "The kids were blown away. They were mesmerized. Bobby talked about doing the right thing and putting God first. He told the kids, 'I don't drink, smoke or believe in pre-marital sex.' It was neat to see a Sacramento King come to club and talk to them like that." According to an article from the local newspaper, Jackson was quite mesmerized himself by the Young Life club. He said, "I wish I had something like this when I was a kid."[67] Not only did Young Life receive a visit from a star, but they managed to affect that player as well.

These stories of success through Jesus Christ on the field of play, Young Life creates a culture of the ruggedness of Christ combined with statements made that Christianity is not for sissies. You can achieve anything in life if you have Christ in your corner. The culture of Young Life promotes an athletic Christianity—a Jesus that calls people with muscles on their body and an eagerness to serve him in the competitive arenas of the world. With photographs of young men participating in football and other rugged sports, the goal of attracting young people to the Christian faith continues to reveal itself. Implicit promises similar to that were presented in the March 1945 issue—that you will become courageous and able to stand up to the "sneer of the gang" if you are a Christian. Perhaps the appeal to strong and athletic young people and famous athletes points to

66. *Relationships*, Winter 2005, 7–8.
67. *Relationships*, Fall 2005, 11.

the emphasis Emile Cailliet described as part of the Young Life ministry. "Whatever the reader's opinion of Young Life's use of key boys as an opening wedge to a large group, it must be clear throughout these pages that, in the last analysis, the Campaign's emphasis *is* on the individual person."[68] Utilizing the cultural message of strength and athleticism becomes a vehicle for sharing the Christian message with large groups of young people.

This attractiveness of Christianity is perpetuated by successful sports figures that proclaim their faith in Jesus Christ through the pages of the *YLM*. Perhaps in an effort to gain a hearing with young people across the country, Jim Rayburn linked himself with successful figures of his day. But strength was not solely found on the playing field. With the representation of American life through football, cowboy shows, and celebrity sports figures reviewed, I will now look at how being a good Christian can strengthen you in the military and influence your patriotism.

If You Are a Good Christian, You Will Be a Good American

The third theme that emerges through my research was and is nationalist in nature. The theme, in essence, states that being American is a Christian ideal. Being American is synonymous with being Christian.[69] This is not a surprising theme given that both the organization and the magazine were started during World War II, a time of heightened patriotism. Articles ranged from how to be a faithful serviceman[70] to remembering Pearl Harbor[71] to fictional stories of life in the military.[72] The cover of the June 1944 issue shows a young man receiving his diploma in front of the American flag.

---

68. Cailliet, *Young Life*, 66. "Fundamentalists for the most part would not see themselves as members of a 'social phenomenon.' Almost all observers have agreed with participants that fundamentalism is in many respects a highly individualized version of Christian faith. The fundamentalists for the most part are church members, but they are not 'churchly' in a sacramental sense . . . To the fundamentalist, participation means being saved" (Marty and Appleby, *Accounting for Fundamentalisms*, 56).

69. Lary May, in the introduction to "Recasting America," alludes to the vision of democracy as redeemed (in comparison to Europe) and as that redeemed ethos America should carry that democracy into battle against fascism and tyranny (May, *Recasting America*, 3).

70. *Young Life* magazine: March 1944, September 1944, May 1956.

71. *Young Life* magazine: December 1944.

72. *Young Life* magazine: March 1951, June 1951, November 1952, December 1952.

As the years progress, the articles on the military evolve into articles discussing political ideals such as how to be a good citizen[73] to issues of communism.[74]

First, let us consider life in the military. In the first issue of the *YLM* (March 1944) there are two articles on servicemen: Robert Thieme of the Air Force and John Daniel of the Navy. Thieme, in directing young people to the source of life, writes a personal message to those in Young Life considering life in the military:

> To you Young Lifers who may be looking forward to service for your country I would say, there are other jungles besides those in the Pacific, you can get bogged down without ever seeing the mud of Italy, you can drift around without being torpedoed into the ocean, you can spin midair without ever touching the control stick

---

73. *Young Life* magazine: July 1958, September 1958.

74. *Young Life* magazine: February 1948, January 1953, March 1953, February 1960, May 1960.

Cultural Expression

of a P-38, so here is the compass directing you to the path, here is solid ground, here is the Navigator, a safe pilot—Jesus Christ who said, "I am the Way, the Truth, and the Life, no man cometh unto the Father, but by me."[75]

John Daniel goes on to recall his history in Young Life and his experience in the Navy. When Daniel was on watch one night while serving, he remembered his time at Young Life camp on Bachman Lake near Dallas, Texas. Recalling the verse "He that hath the Son hath life; and he that hath not the Son of God hath not life," Daniel finally discovered that he did not have joy in his life because he had shut Christ out all together. At that time, on watch in early hours of the morning, Daniel asked Christ to take over his life.[76]

War stories continue. In the May 1944 issue, Henry Vendrick remembers his time at Pearl Harbor when the Japanese attacked. Recalling the peace in his heart during the time of battle, Vendrick gives God the recognition for establishing that peace. Vendrick also gives a personal message to those in the Young Life organization. He states that God does not promise to keep you out of rough places but does promise to go with you. He acknowledges that God helped him the morning of the attack because Jesus loves him, not because he merited it. He notes Jesus loves each one equally and finishes by saying that perhaps he was spared at Pearl Harbor just so he could tell us about Christ who means so much to him.[77]

The October 1944 issue contains an article written by Lt. John Schwab of the Navy. Schwab states, "I really found LIFE, a constant joy and satisfaction when I took Christ on board my ship as the Skipper. Now I have a real destination in life, and the joys that Christ gives me are incomparable with the world."[78] He goes on to say that he used to think Christianity was for old ladies and kids—but he discovered that Christ was for big husky men like him, too. Schwab wanted to be "squared-away" with Christ and discovered that to do so he needed to do two things: first, have a system in place to memorize Scripture, and two, have a system for daily Bible study. In order to grow in knowing the "most fascinating and thrilling love story book in the world" Schwab relates how they would often memorize verses

---

75. *Young Life* magazine, March 1944, 4.
76. Ibid., 5.
77. *Young Life* magazine, May 1944, 5.
78. *Young Life* magazine, October 1944, 9.

while standing in line for food or while standing on watch on the ship. This is one sure way to get "squared-away!"[79]

The September 1945 issue contains an article about men from the Air Force founding a mission agency, Christian Airmen's Missionary Fellowship, thus using their skills to reach people groups around the world. The article includes this description of their work:

> Can't you picture it already? Deep in the heartland of central Africa stands a tall, naked chieftain; beside him, watching the natives clearing out the last bit of underbrush, smiles a tanned young missionary. In his Piper Cub plane he had made this exploratory trip three weeks ago from a distant mission base. He had befriended the chief, and healed his daughter. Now, at last! The shimmering blue skies are all aquiver! A throbbing fills the air. Ten minutes later a twin-engine converted medium bomber roars into a perfect landing.[80]

One of the volunteer airmen, C.W. Rinehart, states that in the post-war era the word printed boldly is opportunity, and he wants to be one whom God uses as hands at the controls of an airplane.[81]

The June 1951 issue offers advice to Christians going into the service in an article titled "Bob Bluejeans Goes to War." The issue begins by stating this might be the first time a serviceman is away from home and Christian support, so offers some advice for handling the pressures of the service while maintaining Christian faith. First, take your stand immediately and let everyone know you are a Christian without doing it in a showy manner. The article recommends kneeling down by your bunk to pray the very first night because if you don't do it the first night you might not develop the habit. Second, be in the habit of reading the Bible. Because it might not be feasible to carry a Bible while on tour, you should be in the habit of memorizing scripture so you can meditate on it any time. Third, be aggressive in your faith. Be friendly, take interest in others, don't complain or pine away for home, keep close to the guys in your outfit, be clean cut in your witness but don't be a hermit, and above all don't gripe! "Be a good soldier for Jesus Christ. Get in the habit of depending on Him for everything you need when temptation hits you, and don't ever let them talk you into compromise—not even one sip, one game, or one word! Keep your life clean

---

79. Ibid.
80. *Young Life* magazine, September 1945, 9.
81. Ibid., 10.

Cultural Expression

and trust God for chances to make your stay with Uncle Sam count in the lives of other guys."[82]

In a May 1956 article we see testimony from a young man entering the Army for the first time, having his new faith tested in an intense atmosphere—boot camp. "Could I just forget about Jesus Christ for the coming years as I had done most of my life previously? Could I leave behind the One Who changed my purpose and place in life so completely only a few short months before? Were the problems as an American G.I. going to be too raw and too many for me to continue to cling to Jesus?"[83] Within a short time this young man met a former Young Life leader who had been drafted, and they would drop down on the rifle range and pull out their New Testament, and then he would have devotional time in a phone booth while others waited in line for breakfast. After having been sent to Europe he realized, "only the strongest and brightest lights continue to be seen in the storm, while the weaker and dimmer ones fail to be noticed. Thus in the armed forces only the sharpest testimonies will remain steadfast in revealing Christ to others."[84] The army became for him a mission field for reaching men for Christ. And in more recent times Young Life continues to be an influential factor for those serving in the armed forces. James Corbin wrote in his letter to the editor,

> I'm currently in Iraq on my third tour as an Infantry officer, and have used the faith I cultivated in Young Life to conquer the fear always residing here. God IS love, and there's no better testimony than when His followers reach out and show it, with no agenda other than pleasing Him. I'm thankful for all I learned in Young Life, and for how God continues to use it today with the next generation.[85]

Given the prominence with which words from servicemen lace the initial issues of the *YLM*, Jim Rayburn gives his opinion and impression of the role of military. We first catch a glimpse in the July 1947 issue where he states: "A Christian who is set on pleasing Jesus Christ in everything he does or says should be the best citizen in his community. Any red-blooded American high school fellow or girl can be a good citizen and yet be obeying

---

82. *Young Life* magazine, June 1951, 5–6.
83. *Young Life* magazine, May 1956, 5.
84. Ibid., 6.
85. *Relationships,* Spring 2010, 3.

and devoted to his Lord at all times."[86] Rayburn's editorial addresses the question of whether you can be a Christian and a patriot at the same time. Rayburn continues in March 1948 to give an example of right and wrong belief and the influence that has on a nation. "When our boys tackled the Japs on far away Pacific islands, they found out they were up against the trickiest, most furious, fanatical enemies that we had ever fought. Those Japs would play dead, then rise up and kill those who approached—they refused to give up—even when the situation was hopeless. They would kill, kill, kill until they themselves were dead. Why? Because they were so heroic and courageous? No! Because they believed wrong."[87]

In the "Marks of a Christian Citizen," ideals for citizenship in allegiance with Christ are set out for us. Five standards for Christian citizenship are outlined: obeying laws, respecting the will of the majority, respecting the rights and opinions of others, hopefulness, and prayer. With these standards in mind, one can be a good Christian and a good citizen simultaneously. This idea is summed up in two standards clearly. Under respecting others' opinion it says, "We expect others to respect our opinions because we regard them as sincere; others have the same right. This is both good Christianity and good citizenship, and therefore Christian citizenship."[88] If a disagreement arises between two parties, it is up to the Christian to arbitrate and cooperate. This can all be accomplished through prayer. "I hope that many people are praying for peace; probably there are. Christian citizens will represent a tremendous power for peace when they harness their petitions to God regardless of creed or faith."[89] Good citizenship is subsumed in Christianity.

With stories of servicemen living faithfully in the military, combined with the opinion of the founder of Young Life, it is clear that in the *YLM* being a good Christian means being a good American. Obviously those citizens

---

86. *Young Life* magazine, July 1947, 4. "In the 1940s and 1950s communism stood not only for atheism, totalitarianism, and a nuclear threat from abroad, but also at least intimated the menace of atheistic secularism promoted by big government at home. During the early Cold War American patriotism was at a peak and not surprisingly often took on a 'Manichean' quality. On the 'good' side of this dichotomy was 'The American Way of Life,' often associated with family values and a 'Christian,' or increasingly 'Judeo-Christian' heritage... Another significant area where explicitly evangelical influence was growing was the American military" (Marsden, *Fundamentalism and American Culture*, 239–240).

87. *Young Life* magazine, March 1948, 4.

88. *Young Life* magazine, July 1956, 11.

89. Ibid., 16.

of other countries, whether the naked chieftain of Africa or the murderous Japanese, do not believe correctly and it is up to those faithful Americans to show them the way. But times change and military threats shift. As the years pass, Young Life's emphasis on military life shifts to a focus on politics and nationality. We now will examine articles that illustrate the nationalist vision of Young Life in order to discern their implicit messages.

The chief political rhetoric focused on communism and its political force throughout the world. The first article written on this subject was titled "Is America Going Communist?" and appeared in the February 1948 issue and written by Dr. S. Richey Kamm, head of the history and social science department at Wheaton College, Illinois. In a two-part series, Dr. Kamm gave an overview of the background events that led to communism, discussing the philosophies of Marx and Engels and the influence of Lenin.[90] Kamm's argument, found in the second article, states: "By our insistence upon the tentative truths of science as the only basis of thinking and acting, we have cut off the present generation of American youth from the eternal and abiding truths of our Hebrew-Christian heritage."[91] He argues that in cutting off young people from these basic Christian understandings, we have robbed America of the reality of sin and the necessity of redemption that shows the authority of God and the atoning work of Christ.[92]

Five years later, the January and March issues of 1953 reveal a similar thread pertaining to Christianity in America and the "threat" of communism. These articles centered on the growing population of communists in France, and urged that missionaries be sent there. The article states, "We believe Christianity is the great bulwark against Communism. Democracy as we know it in America is a product of Christianity. It is not enough to offer Europe democracy. We must offer her Christianity." In order to push back the threatening shadow of communism, American and French Christian witnesses were needed to give France an opportunity.[93]

In a preceding article discussing the positive components of Young Life club, issues pertaining to communism surface in a description of a

90. Kamm, "Is America Going Communist?" February 1948, 9.

91. Kamm, "Is America Going Communist?" March 1948, 26.

92. Ibid. "In this view, America is God's chosen nation—the covenanted people, as the Puritans suggested. This view is drawn from the Old Testament and is directed toward culture-building rather than culture-avoiding. America, says this covenantal view, has been blessed with prosperity because she has been an essentially Christian nation" (Marsden, *Religion and American Culture*, 96).

93. *Young Life* magazine, March 1953, 7–8.

conversation between three high school girls. Having gone for sodas after school, these girls are discussing the possibility of attending Young Life club that night. The discussion moves from Young Life's dissimilarity of church and the basics of the Bible, to Young Life's positive influence on youth society. The article concludes with Gay's statement, "Another advantage of Young Life is this too, kids, America's high school kids like us can really fight Communism as we become aware of God. Communism undermines Christianity and the Bible which is 'the rock on which our Republic rests' according to Robert E. Lee."[94]

A similar sentiment was reflected in an article discussing the arms race between the United States and Russia in the December 1957 issue. Russia, having launched Sputnik, challenged the United States to a "race" and the US responded. But the author muses that "it is in the realm of ideas and truth, in faith and morals and spiritual teachings about God and his Christ that could make America really great."[95]

Finally, in an article that appeared in the February 1960 issue, the opinion of the spiritual nature of democracy and communism is revealed. Through the support of the Kresge foundation, Young Life staff was given the opportunity to interview people who had crossed from east to west in the city of Berlin. The article, centering around the trip of eleven Young Life leaders to Berlin Germany, includes quotes from Germans who had passed through the "Hole in the Iron Curtain." "We believe that the constant stream of refugees is proof enough. Men do not escape from freedom. They only escape to it."[96] A German who was interviewed said this, "The divided condition of Germany is a result of a revolt against God, not only by the Soviets, but by our own people from the time of Hitler. It is Satanic in origin. The innocent suffer with the guilty. But the most innocent of all, Jesus Christ, suffers the most."[97] The article reveals the opinion that it was believed communism was Satanic, therefore implying that democracy was Christian.

But there are also current examples of the connection between a military understanding and Christianity in the Young Life organization. In an editorial from the December 1987 issue of *Relationships*, president Doug Burleigh equates volunteers in Young Life to an army that is laboring in the

94. *Young Life* magazine, January 1955, 14.
95. *Young Life* magazine, December 1957, 19.
96. *Young Life* magazine, February 1960, 30.
97. Ibid.

trenches trying to reach young people with the news of Christ. After reviewing statistics of the number of high school students not being touched by the Young Life ministry he states, "*We need nothing less than a veritable army of staff and volunteers to go to America's 22,500 senior and many more junior high schools to love kids boldly for Jesus Chris.*"[98] Burleigh concludes his editorial by sounding a rally call for more adults to join Young Life in reaching out to students in their local communities, near their local schools. "That's the kind of petition that will indeed 'shake the gates of hell,' release God's army to reach out to kids, and bring delight to the heart of our Lord."[99]

The military language continues in an editorial written by president Denny Rydberg titled "Getting Offensive" in the January/February 1997 issue of the *YLM* he states:

> I can see the results. We attack, we break down the gates, we bring kids into the light, the Good News is shared, kids meet Christ and life is different. If we don't, life is the same for the millions of kids in the United States and around the world who have never had an opportunity to hear a clear presentation about Jesus Christ and who have never been given an opportunity to say "Yes" to the Lord. Someone has to attack the fortress. That someone is us.[100]

Rydberg, reiterating the goal of quadrupling the ministry in ten years, communicated that going from 6 percent to 25 percent of middle schools and high schools could only be done by the guidance of the Holy Spirit, and that Young Life staff does so for Christ's sake. Rydberg wanted Young Life to go deep, wide and long. Going deep was understood to be "penetrating at an even greater level every school in which we already have a presence... Going deep is not being content with what we've done in the past. It's a plan for the future." Rydberg wanted to attack the gates of schools locally. Wide was understood to be the regional plan. Long was understood to be the whole division of Young Life. Rydberg closes by saying "Let's all get even more offensive for the cause of Christ and the love of kids."[101] Military language, then, shapes the outlook and perspective of the Young Life ministry as they look to go on the offensive for the Lord.

The Fall 1995 issue of the *YLM* included an article titled, "From Serving his Country to Serving his Country's Youth" that focused on a naval

---

98. *Relationships*, December 1987, 2. Italics in original.
99. Ibid.
100. *Relationships*, January/February 1997, 3.
101. Ibid., 3 & 16.

officer named Robbie Robertson. Robertson came to the Christian faith as an adult after having been introduced to Young Life through a friend who was a lawyer. A graduate of the Naval Academy with twenty years of service as an engineer, this friend was able to introduce Robertson to some new things in terms of the Christian faith. Robertson states, "He showed me some things about Christianity that I didn't know were possible–the ability to have fun, be an exciting person and still be a Christian. And one day, I told the Lord I wanted what my friend had."[102] The article goes on to state that though he attended great schools and traveled the world "as a representative of the strongest nation on earth, he knew something was missing in his life." Robertson now works with young people so that they don't go through the same things he did. "When you go through a good part of your life without being a Christian then you feel really strong about the need to keep high school kids from doing that, so they don't need to go through their 20s and 30s like I did—without Christ."[103]

In an article titled, "The Call of Duty" tells the story of an article on Rear Admiral Robert Burt, Chief of the Navy Chaplains. Rear Admiral Burt remembers when he was invited to Young Life club by upper classmen when he was a sophomore football player. "So that night I went to my first Young Life [club], and I was hooked. It was awesome. What I really appreciated was the fun they had. I was very excited that the Christian faith was presented in an environment of enthusiasm, energy and excitement and we still had a few minutes to pause and give the spirit of God the chance to speak to our hearts. I never missed a meeting."[104] Solidifying his Christian faith at Frontier Ranch (Young Life camp), Chaplain Burt credited his relationship with his Young Life leader Jack Loy. When asked if the paradigm of relational ministry fit his work as a Navy chaplain, Burt states:

> Most definitely. I encourage chaplains to get involved in the life of their command–do physical training with Marines, hike the hills with them, gain their respect. Chaplains have many opportunities to sit down and have what I call extraordinary access. When a sailor is out on the deck of a ship at 9 or 10 at night thinking about life, a chaplain can walk up and engage him in conversation and give guidance. What an incredible opportunity we have. That's

---

102. *Relationships*, Fall 1995, 23.
103. Ibid., 23–24.
104. *Relationships*, Spring 2007, 17.

Cultural Expression

the whole reason we do it—we care about them and want them to know God loves them.[105]

Denny Rydberg utilizes language of and appreciation of military language and understanding. In an editorial titled, "Lessons Jose Taught Me," Rydberg reflects on the life of Jose Reynaldo Sisneros. He was a special friend of Young Life who died and Rydberg reflects on his experience at the funeral of this friend.

> I came away reminded of what's important. I want all of us to remember that fancy really doesn't matter. That fancy is tremendously over-rated. That life can have great meaning in the simple and the plain, in the company of the Lord, family and friends. It is my hope and prayer that we not become so busy in doing good that we miss the best . . . And I want people to know when they gather around our caskets that we served proudly in the war. For some of us, that means serving in the military. For all of us, it means battling proudly in the war being waged for the lives of kids. Jose Reynaldo Sisneros, I am grateful for the lessons you taught me in the middle of a snowstorm. May you rest in peace.[106]

Young Life reinforces a message of attractiveness for young people in being good citizens and following Christ simultaneously. Through the stories of servicemen, the opinions of Young Life staff, and focus of political values, Young Life creates the message that to be a good American is to be Christian, and to be Christian is to be a good American. In the May 1955 issue, a telegram from the governor of the state of Washington is included. The telegram states that the governor, Arthur B. Langlie, welcomed the Young Life Campaign to the city of Olympia as they gathered for a banquet at the Olympic Hotel. "We wish, as you do, that every high school student in our nation could have the opportunity of hearing and understanding the truth of Jesus Christ and that thousands of teenagers, yet un-reached, could have the opportunity to experience the joy of finding the way of life and the key to happiness."[107] It is of little surprise that political leaders would join Young Life in promoting good Christian citizenship.

A theme, running through articles of military and politics, links patriotism to faithfulness. Christianity is summed up in the democratic freedom of the United States, and that message is carried throughout the world.

---

105. Ibid., 17–18.
106. *Relationships*, Spring 2002, 2.
107. *Young Life* magazine, May 1955, 17.

The culminating message of the attractiveness of Christianity is contained in stories heard from Young Life camp. The camp environment enables campers to discover the beauty of creation, experience the ruggedness of faith by hiking mountains and jumping off snow cliffs, and faith that supports one's patriotic values can be experienced at Young Life camp. Let us now look at the message and foundation of Young Life camp set forth in the magazine.

Young Life Camp: Giving You the Best Week of Your Life

From early on, the Young Life Campaign positioned itself to offer a premier week of camp to young people involved in the ministry. They used camp as a promotional tool to attract young people to the organization, and pitched the phrase "you'll have the best week of your life."[108]

In "Camping Clicks" (September 1944) an article written by Wally Howard, we are given the first insight to camping in the Young Life ministry "If kids were given a vote on the Young Life activity which they like the most—a choice between week by week Young Life Clubs, occasional mass meetings in hotel ballrooms, or the summer camps—first choice would be a boisterous cheer for camp . . . You see it's not the rough and ready variety of camping that clears a patch of ground for a pup tent—it is camping deluxe!"[109] The messages given by Young Life leaders were often discussed informally at night on the bunks, and out of those discussions came decisions to give Jesus Christ a try and a new desire to witness to the "gang" back home.[110] These first summers of camp, spent on properties rented by Young Life, set the foundation for Young Life's camping ministry in years to come.[111]

---

108. "The reason we have beautiful and well-equipped camps is to proclaim the gospel of Jesus Christ in a setting that speaks well of Him. The reason we provide campers with good food, good housing, excellent swimming pools, good ropes courses, fun water programs, Hondas and exceptional entertainment is to build an attractive platform from which we proclaim our message" (Miller, *Back to the Basics*, 141).

109. *Young Life* magazine, September 1944, 5–6.

110. Ibid., 15.

111. Rayburn and the early leaders of Young Life understood young people could be persuaded by the experiences they had if it was done to their standard of excellence and uniqueness. Mark Senter summarizes the impact of the early Young Life vision. "From that vision for ministry came the entirely new concept of resort camping to reach

Cultural Expression

Star Ranch, purchased in the summer of 1946, became the first official Young Life camp in the organization. Sitting at the foot of Cheyenne Mountain, Colorado, it promised to be "the most outstanding young people's camp in the country" (July 1946, back cover).

"Just remember this, gang, Star Ranch was given to us by the Lord and He has worked in a wonderful way to equip and maintain this beautiful place— all for you. Ask Sonny Price, Sammy Adams, Dick Simmons, Dee Ogden,

---

students for Christ. Camp began playing a key role in the evangelization of non-churched young people. Students came by the bus load, first to the Star Ranch and other Young Life camps in Colorado, and then to facilities located in picturesque locations across the continent . . . the vision shaped the ministry" (Senter, *The Coming Revolution in Youth Ministry*, 74).

Poncho Page or Ed Whitten–they saw the Lord work at Star Ranch!"[112] During the 1950s the focus on Young Life camp became a main theme running throughout the magazine.

Beginning in October 1950, and repeating at least once a year through 1960, the magazine featured photographs of camp and the imperative that is repeated consistently throughout: "see for themselves why kids say that a week spent at Star Ranch or Star Lodge is 'the best week of your whole life.'" The photographs accompanying this article show the Star Lodge ranch main entrance, three young people riding horseback, and a group of young people swimming and sunbathing at Lodge's pool.[113] In an issue the next year, March 1951, two of those photographs re-appear—the photograph of horseback riding and the swimming pool scene. This issue is accompanied by these words: "Silver Cliff Ranch [formerly Star Lodge] nestles beneath cathedral-like cliffs . . . Past its door flows Chalk Creek where you will want to try your hand at trout fishing . . . Through the grounds flows the hottest spring water in the entire state, heating the Lodge and warming the pool so that outdoor swimming is a delight at any time of year . . . and the sixteen well-constructed log cabins can accommodate an ample crowd."[114]

Attention to a specific camp depended on the year. Early articles of camp featured those properties that were purchased in Colorado. The articles featured photographs and lists of popular activities at camp, as well as features from young people who had come to the Christian faith while at camp. "The best week of your life" was often connected to the adventuresome spirit of camping with Young Life. Here is a description of Roundup Lodge [Frontier Ranch] after it was purchased for Young Life in the spring of 1951:

> The property comprises 2500 acres of timberland in the San Isabel National Forest . . . There are 55 buildings, 34 of them guest cabins, the others filling every conceivable purpose. Separate buildings are set aside for dining, recreation, handcraft, library, photography, and so on. A standard 75-foot warm water swimming pool

---

112. *Young Life* magazine, August 1946, 26. "The key to running a successful camp was quality. In a time when lean-tos, tent houses, and meager surroundings were synonymous with Christian camps, Jim insisted on excellence. He'd say, 'Who started the idea that Christians ought to have the seat of their pants in patches, or that we ought to have camps in tents? We talk about the King of Kings; let's act like he's the one in charge! We're gonna get the classiest camps in the country'" (Rayburn III, *Dance, Children, Dance*, 74).

113. *Young Life* magazine, October 1950, 12–13.

114. *Young Life* magazine, March 1951, 14.

vies with the string of fine riding horses (there are more than 100 of them!) for interest. Two surfaced tennis courts, three baseball diamonds, basketball courts, volleyball court, badminton court, an outdoor amphitheatre seating 300, and Sunset Point barbeque and picnic grounds are other features.[115]

With a description like this, it is easy to see how a young person could have the greatest week of their life when they are surrounded by activities and beauty as described above. With a setting like Frontier Ranch with warm swimming pools, horses and activities, Young Life was also intent on shaping the greatest week by providing compelling entertainment and delicious food.

In the article "Colorado is Calling," Young Life style camp is explained in an effort to attract young people to camp that summer "Young Life style means a style all our own. There's nothing else quite like it in a summer camp. There's a full program every week of athletic competition, sight seeing, the goofiest entertainment in the world, eating 'high on the hog,' friendly helpful roundups, and lots of good old 'fellowship' with kids from far and wide."[116] The article continues with photographs from two camps, Star Ranch and Frontier Ranch, both in Colorado. With pictures of sprawling camp property, a young woman eating barbeque, and young people lining up outside of a building under expansive sky, the description of the pictures revealed their personal understanding. "Star Ranch's buildings and lawns make it known as the 'country club of camping.' Frontier Ranch is a fabulous cluster of colorful western buildings, 57 in all."[117] Further description extols the deluxe nature of Star Ranch where you can find all you need in basketball, volleyball, swimming, shuffleboard, hiking and climbing. At Frontier you could climb to the top of the Continental Divide, take an overnight hike, or visit a ghost town.[118] The article concludes with a photograph of three young women with their heads down, moping, be-

---

115. *Young Life* magazine, June 1951, 12–13. "Frontier Ranch became Jim's lover. She restored him, rebuilt him, and sent him off to battle with a soft kiss. His residence there was known as the Lookout. It was the only place he ever called home. Those summers spent in the Lookout were the happiest times of his life. The awesome beauty of the place seemed an appropriate match to Jim's awesome faith and lifestyle. It was wonderful to see my father so fulfilled. Life had thrown a lot of problems in his direction, and the Lookout seemed to be God's way of providing him a special refuge" (Rayburn III, *Dance, Children, Dance*, 103).

116. *Young Life* magazine, April 1952, 5.

117. Ibid.

118. Ibid., 6–7.

cause they do not want to leave camp. "Of course, who wants to leave God's country?"[119] A similar article appears in the April 1953 edition, although different photographs accompany it. The accompanying pictures include a group of horseback riders taking in the scenery, a group of hikers resting in between cliffs, a group playing water basketball, and a group singing around a piano.[120]

In the mid to late 1950s, attention shifted and was given almost exclusively to Malibu, the Young Life camp in Canada. The first article on Malibu appeared in the March 1954 issue, featuring statistics and information about the camp as well as enticing photographs. The first photograph shows a group of young people on a boat holding up fish caught on a lake that is overshadowed by towering mountains. On the following page, photographs show the boat that guests must take from Vancouver in order to access camp, as well as a scene of young people diving and swimming in the lake. The article describes the route one must take to get to camp—under bridges, past glaciers, and traversing inlets. Then it describes a "teenager's paradise"—two great inns, cabins, boat docks, golf course, tennis courts, stores and shops. "In addition to the usual camping activities offered by Young Life at its Colorado ranches, Malibu will offer water skiing, boat trips, wonderful fishing (a thirty pound salmon is not uncommon), and a spectacular variety of mountains to climb for those who go in for such rugged adventure."[121] The June 1954 issue follows up the first experiences of Malibu with excerpts from letters received from young people.

The issue, combined with a photograph of a young man and woman canoeing on the lake, includes comments regarding Malibu as the greatest place a teenager could go. The following page shows three photographs of Jim Rayburn at Malibu speaking to groups of young people.[122] The 1954 focus on camp concludes with a September feature of pictures from Malibu showing boating and fishing, as well as boys eating in their cabin in contrast to girls primping in front of a mirror in their cabin.[123]

119. Ibid., 8.
120. *Young Life* magazine, April 1953, 12–13.
121. *Young Life* magazine, March 1954, 15. "A week with Jim and his crazy, talented followers was akin to a week on Fantasy Island. He did everything with a verve and zest that showed his love of life. It was contagious, this constant urge to stretch every nerve and muscle, to go beyond the mundane patterns of life, and Jim's growing staff caught his spirit of adventure" (Rayburn III, *Dance, Children, Dance*, 74).
122. *Young Life* magazine, June 1954, 11–13.
123. Ibid., 16–17.

Cultural Expression

Some of the 100 "charter" campers at Malibu stop off at the totum pole in their tour of the grounds between mountains and the water of Princess Louisa Inlet.
Cameras are needed to help describe the unbelievable beauty of Malibu. These kids are prepared. At right, evening round-up with Bob Mitchell, Jim Rayburn.

The March 1958 and April 1959 issues are almost entirely dedicated to summer camping. The March 1958 issue is written from the perspective of a camera named Mr. Peeper. The April 1959 issue is written from the perspective of a horse named Goldie. Both reports feature "memories" from the two characters and their experience at camp that summer, and both feature photographs and descriptions of what one will find at Young Life camp, focusing on water sports, horseback riding, athletics, entertainment, eating, socializing, and roundups.

All of these descriptions have been summed up in the testimony of young people and their experience at camp as described in the January and August issues of 1956. In the January issue, an article written by a young man who had volunteered for the work crew at Frontier Ranch in Colorado. He describes his first encounter with the scenery of the Rocky Mountains and his feeling of God's majesty and his insignificance. Describing his view of the land of Colorado from the top of Mt. Princeton he asks this, "If I'm so small, how can God, who made all of this, care for me?" Then he relates what he feels is the main point: God created human beings to have fellowship with him and to talk to him. Quoting Romans 6:23, he focuses on the fact that Jesus died for each of us individually and asks, "Can you still wonder whether or not He cares for you?"[124]

124. *Young Life* magazine, January 1956 16–17.

The August issue is comprised of two testimonies from young women who attended Frontier Ranch. The first simply describes a daily schedule of what happens at camp and her favorite activities such as the athletic competitions between North and South and the trip to the ghost town. The highlight for her was meeting young people from around the country as well as all the activity that was scheduled throughout the day. The second testimony describes a camp experience from the perspective of a dating relationship. She met him while at Young Life camp, and "Deep down inside she knew that it would last forever. He would always be loyal to her and never let her down. She could depend on him. His love was constant, something she had never experienced before." Her description is of Christ, the one introduced to her by talks during "Roundups" and explained by other kids at camp. "Jean has found a lifelong friend who will always love her ... kind of like going steady, only much better."[125] With these testimonies, we catch a glimpse of what young people took away from their time at camp: stunning beauty and multiple activities to hold your attention and give you a sense of adventure, as well as an introduction to a man who will love you individually and forever.

In an article titled "The Best Week of My Life," high school student Mark Pattee of Colorado describes the welcome he receives when arriving at Malibu Young Life camp in British Columbia. He states, "I loved the welcome, the band coming out to play for us and the water skiers. The people on the dock seemed so friendly and open and happy to see us, I couldn't believe it. I cruised off the ship and all the work crew[126] girls were jumping and laughing and singing and grabbing and kissing me. And I thought, 'Hey, this couldn't be better!' When I finally got through the line, my mouth was tired from smiling so much."[127] It is no wonder young people experience the best week of their life at Young Life camp when a young man is welcomed to camp with a line of young women laughing and singing and offering kisses as you arrive. If a young person is to enter into the family of Christ while at Young Life camp, the organization certainly situates itself well to celebrate that entrance.

---

125. *Young Life* magazine, August 1956, 6–7.

126. The Young Life work crew consists of high school students who volunteer one month to work at a Young Life camp. They are usually students who have become Christians and desire to give back to the ministry. Young Life has a similar program for college age students called Summer Staff.

127. Young Life, *Focus on Youth*, Fall 1976, 4.

Cultural Expression

Over the years, the *YLM* featured articles and insights from young people who had attended Young Life camp. An article titled "It'll be the Greatest Week in Your Life!" featured journal entries from a camper at Young Life camp. At the beginning of the article the author states, "That's what we promise kids about their time at a Young Life summer camp. They'll water ski, parasail, ride Honda's, meet new friends, and more. But often the most significant things remembered have to do with their personal experience of faith in Jesus Christ."[128]

Camp also becomes a second Eden, according to a Young Life staff person in a letter to the editor in the Fall 2005 issue. She concludes, "What Young Life camp does, ever so sneakily, is this: it reclaims humor, laughter, good memories and unconditional acceptance. It challenges kids with the fact that a better way to live is through purity, passion and forgiveness. Camps says this is the way life should have been, and you're going back to a life that could be better, if only you remember what you lived this past week."[129] The life you experience at Young Life camp is the way 'life should have been.' And if you remember what you experience at camp, then life will be better when you return home again. Young Life camp is the reflection of what life should be like.

Young Life camp has been a long-standing feature within the *YLM* beginning in the early days of the organization in the 1940s. From the beginning, Young Life stated that you would experience "the best week of your life" at Young Life, and that message continues in current issues of the *YLM*. However, other emphases are included in these current issues regarding the relationship between counselor and student at Young Life camp, perspectives from young people attending camp, and experiences from Young Life camps outside of the United States.

Bob Mitchell, former president of Young Life, reflects on his understanding and experience with Young Life camps in the June/July 1987[130] issue of the *YLM*. Mitchell reflects it was Jim Rayburn's understanding that when adults and kids did things together—adventurous things—young people were more receptive to the gospel. Because of the success of reaching

---

128. *Relationships*, Summer 1994, 20–22.

129. *Relationships*, Fall, 2005, 3.

130. The front cover of this 1987 issue of the *YLM* states, "Activities at Young Life camps, like parasailing, provide an interesting context in which to grow relationships between teens and adults, teens and teens, and ultimately, teens and God" (*Relationships*, June/July 1987, 2).

young people through the venue of Young Life camps, Mitchell believed these camps would be around for a long time. Mitchell goes on to state,

> It's not that we want to build a huge empire of camps. Though we would rather not own a whole lot of properties, we have found it difficult to rent or lease facilities that fit well with the Young Life style of camping and proclamation of the gospel. We don't think camps have to be plush, but we've found it beneficial for kids to have a comfortable place to sleep, an exciting recreational facility and a good counseling and communication situation. But our camps are not about physical and tangible things. Basically camp is kids and leaders doing things together. It is getting to know each other better and having the opportunity to get to know Jesus better in the process.[131]

In a June 1989 article titled "A Camping Ministry in Africa," perspectives of Young Life camping in Africa are shared by Martie Sheffer, longtime staff person in Young Life. Sheffer discusses the drawbacks that were encountered when considering planning a Young Life camp in Kenya: "We've no money. No camp-sites. No songbooks. No musical instruments—well maybe one well-worn guitar. No game equipment. No cooks. No program staff and no work crew. No trained counselors except us. No anything. . . . Our trainees learned the value of what has made Young Life camping effective in the United States: counselor involvement—counselors contacting kids where they are, bringing them to camp, being with them at all times, and doing all the camp activities with them." Sheffer states that Young Life camp properties in the United States are a great asset to the ministry but he concludes with what he believes are the most important things to consider: "Winning souls is the work of God, and it can happen anywhere. I saw that in Africa."[132]

Denny Rydberg, in an editorial from the Summer 1994 issue, understood Young Life camp as not simply a place for adults and young people to build relationships, but a place for young people to be cleansed by the love of God.

> There are places in our country where hundreds of kids experience deep down clean every week of the summer. It's called Young Life camp. And the showers are on full-time. Kids can come with all kinds of heartaches, headaches, and regrets and cast their cares on

131. Ibid., 4.
132. *Relationships*, June 1989, back cover.

the Lord and He does what He has done for humans for centuries. He cares for them. These kids leave camp different than when they came.[133]

Thus, Young Life camp is the place the forgiveness through Jesus Christ is offered to young people and they leave refreshed.

A similar understanding of camp being the place where students experience and reflect a change in life was also illustrated in an editorial by Rydberg titled "Year of the Lord's Favor." In this editorial, Rydberg reflects on the status of young people today. Noting that some are rich in material but poor in spirit, some are trying to fill their souls with whatever they can find. He also notes some are prisoners of abuse, poverty, or grief. He finds they are captive to their decisions and addictions. Rydberg then states,

> In the middle of all of this, we in Young Life come proclaiming the Year of the Lord's Favor . . . Although kids meet Christ in many settings in Young Life, we can see this transformation[134] take place at a Young Life camp. We watch a group of kids arrive at camp. We see emptiness in their eyes, despair on their faces. As the week goes by, they might express their hostility or their mourning. But gradually they meet Jesus, and their lives change. Beauty, gladness and praise replace their ashes, mourning and despair.[135]

The idea of camp being the greatest week of your life was reflected in a letter to the editor from a high school student named Wade Atkins. He states, "One of my best friends and I were invited to a Young Life camp last summer. It not only sounded cool, but I really was interested in going. My best friend and I were on the bus that headed to Sharp Top Cove, Georgia, this summer to experience the best week of our lives."[136] Atkins goes on to account that everything he experienced was perfect: rides, club, and even the food. He recalled that he enjoyed hanging out with friends while at camp, but he also started a relationship with Christ while there. "Second, I started a true relationship with God. That was truly amazing. I learned so much

133. *Relationships*, Summer 1994, 4.

134. This idea of transformation is not relegated to young people alone. In a letter to the editor in the Winter 2009 issue, Tom and Pam Huissen recall bringing adults to Young Life camp as guests. Though one guest was skeptical about the impact a camp could have on young people, "By the end of the week his own life was being transformed! He went back to his area on fire for the Lord and for getting more involved with Young Life!" (*Relationships*, Winter 2009, 3)

135. *Relationships*, Winter 2003, 2–3.

136. *Relationships*, Fall 2006, 3.

about Him while I was there. Some of the things I learned I didn't really want to, like that I'll never be good enough for God. But, I also learned that He is all-forgiving. No matter what I do, He will forgive me and still love me. His love is unconditional. This love is something that we, as His people, need to show more."[137]

In an article titled "Treated Like Royalty," the centrality of the young person is highlighted. A camper named Coshawn Jackson reflected on his time at camp.

> I just want to thank you for bringing God into my life. The week for me was the best experience and feelings I've had in a long time. Thank you for making me understand more about God in my life. Just having a relationship with Him is the best thing in my life and it's just because of you that my life has changed. Also, thanks for the best food[138] I've had in a while. I really appreciate you guys working hard to please us. Thank you for the time you took with me to help me understand. I will always be grateful for that.[139]

Illustrating the idea of treating kids at Young Life camp like royalty, a story was shared in the Fall 2006 issue of the *YLM*. Recalling Young Life camp in Dar es Salaam in Tanzania, the story recounted how young people were welcomed—especially one camper named Michael. It is a tradition at Young Life camp to welcome campers as they come to camp in grand fashion; in this case kids were welcomed by Young Life staff as well as a brass wedding band. The last bus to arrive that day only had one camper on it—his name was Michael. The story recalls,

> We always ask the question to leaders in training: "Would you do everything the same if it was for just one kid?" Well that's just what the leaders did for Michael. One hundred work crew and a brass band greeted him, put him on their shoulders and carried him into camp and joined the other 178 kids at the camp. Three days later, Michael began a relationship with Jesus Christ. "And he was carried into the kingdom of God." Was it worth it for just one kid? I think I know what Michael would say.[140]

---

137. Ibid.

138. In a study on Young Life camps being conducted by Dr. Justin Barrett there is an initial tie between the food served at camp and the likelihood of a young person to make a commitment to Christ (Conference paper, January 2009).

139. *Relationships*, Spring/Summer 2000, 4–5.

140. *Relationships*, Fall 2006, 17.

Young Life camp becomes a place not only where young people are treated with great care and special treatment, but it also becomes a place for deep conversation. Mike Ashburn[141] reflected on the shift in conversations he was having with young people at camp. He states, "My general observation is that kids today know a little bit about a lot—shallow information—just enough to be dangerous. I do see kids coming to camp more intellectually prepared to hear a lot more, especially in terms of theology. I'm discussing topics that five years ago would have seemed like opening a can of worms. But now I'll bring up evolution, I'll talk about the law of thermodynamics, we'll discuss the Holy Spirit and the Trinity. Kids today are quoting philosophers, some I've never even heard of, and they're intrigued with other religions."[142] He goes on to recall a conversation with a young man while sitting on the back porch at Malibu (Young Life's camp in British Columbia, Canada). The young man was stating that he had chosen to be a little bit of many religions: a bit Buddhist, a bit Hindu, and a bit Christian. Ashburn closes by reflecting the importance of Young Life camp as a place for relationships. "Our young people today have access to a lot of information, but are they any smarter? I think that the end of the story is that it isn't about religion . . . it's still about relationships."[143]

With activities such as horseback riding, snow jumping, hiking, and water sports combined with great food and entertaining programming, Young Life camp positioned itself to be the premier resort for high school young people. In featuring camp within the pages of the magazine, Young Life was able to present the arena that set them apart from other youth ministry programs of their day. Camp is a summation of their ministry: attractive, athletic, full of traditional American activities like barbeques and horseback riding—provide the perfect environment to present the one whom they find most attractive of all, Jesus Christ.

Conclusion

Recounting the stories and messages of the *YLM* between the years 1944–1960, I set forth the themes that emerge from this written text. In order to analyze this text to the extent needed to provide the foundational message

141. Mike 'Ash' Ashburn filled the position of special assistant to the president until his retirement in 2007.

142. *Relationships*, Spring 2002, 6.

143. Ibid.

of the organization for future study, I will utilize resources from the field of American religious history. There are elements of American culture threading their way through the stories accounted for, and church history sheds some light on the position Young Life holds. As we begin to compare the Young Life message with that of the historical American church, we begin to outline the implicit beliefs Young Life holds about God.

In this chapter I have analyzed the *Young Life Magazine* (1944–1960) as a way to understand the historical positioning of Young Life and have argued that Young Life's vision of the Christian faith is one of an attractive, athletic, nationalist faith that found its culmination in a week at Young Life camp. Through the *YLM*, the Young Life organization declared the manliness and love of Jesus, and sought to present that in the most attractive way. Through stories of the athletic achievement of stars such as Gil Dodds, Don Moumaw or Roy Rogers, themes of the attractive strength of Christ are relayed. Through stories of military life and issues nationalist in nature, the theme of being a good American and a good Christian are laid out. All of these stories were experienced at Young Life camp through adventure, entertainment, and excellence in camping. I have looked at the context of *YLM* in the mid-twentieth century as a means for framing future study of Young Life within the Holland Area. In establishing the themes and patterns of stories told, I will be able to compare contemporary stories of Young Life in order to mark any changes or similarities that may remain today. The foundational stories of Young Life may be linked to the personality of its founder Jim Rayburn, or the political or rhetorical emphasis of the day. Nonetheless, *YLM* communicated an interest in an attractive Christian faith for young people.

5
Conclusions and Recommendations

THIS WORK HAS SOUGHT to investigate the theological foundations of the Young Life ministry utilizing historic documents of the organization and observations of local ministry. Despite my past experience with Young Life, I was still driven to find out, "What does Young Life believe?" As I began my research I was looking for an articulation of theological tenets that have given shape and currently guide the organization, and I found that Young Life articulates a culturally nuanced version of Christianity. As I began this thesis I framed my discussion in practical theology and specifically on the work of Elaine Graham. Graham argued that Christian communities generate theology as they live out expressions of Christian truth-claims in their life together. She argued that theology is thus enacted and embodied in Christian practice. As I conclude this thesis I return once again to the questions Graham raised as she entered into her own study of practical theology and Christian communities. She asked,

> In the face of the collapse of the 'grand narrative' of modernity, what values may now inform purposeful Christian action and vision? Do Christian truth-claims make any coherent sense amidst the multiple narratives of the public domain? Can Christian communities respond to changing values and competing world-views construct a self-understanding that will sustain them through the challenges of the new millennium? These questions all concern the nature of Christian presence in the world, informed by traditions and conventions of faith, yet seeking anew to respond to the challenges of human need and ultimate value.[1]

1. Graham, *Transforming Practice*, 2.

It is my belief that "in the face of the collapse of the grand-narrative of modernity" the Young Life organization in the United States has struggled to make the transition from the truth-claims that formed the foundation of their ministry in the 1940s to the challenges of the new millennium they are facing today. Do the Christian themes that shaped the Young Life organization in 1941 still maintain and communicate the theological position they desire young people to garner today? I argue that Young Life is foundationally challenged in responding to the changing values and competing world-views they are coming up against in terms of providing theological belonging for young people. However, I believe that Young Life, if they are willing to adapt, have strong and innovative practices that give them the capacity for reaching young people today. As I have stated, Young Life has maintained a consistent cultural message of an attractive, strong Christianity that is relayed through incarnational and relational ministry over the decades of their outreach. I discovered through my research that Young Life has consistently argued for a praxis of ministry that begins with an understanding of incarnational theology with the intention of providing an environment for unreached young people to feel welcome. Young Life has also consistently articulated their intention to focus attention on the person of Jesus Christ—not from a theological perspective but a relational one–believing that an encounter with the attractive person of Christ will lead young people to the faith. But I believe Young Life must come to terms with the question Graham posits in the introduction to her work when she asks, "Is it possible to maintain the *boundaries* of coherent community with binding truth-claims whilst remaining open to the *horizons* of diversity and provisionality?"[2] Is Young Life capable of maintaining the boundaries of their strong emphasis of reaching young people for Christ who have never heard of Jesus before yet remain open to diverse situations that may arise when working with teenagers? Are they able to maintain consistent messages of Christianity while being flexible enough to answer the questions young people are asking today of faith?

In this conclusion I will reiterate how I approached this project and the methodology utilized for the task of understanding and articulating the theological foundation of the Young Life organization. I will again emphasize the main arguments in each chapter in efforts to summarize my argument and will evaluate the Young Life organization in light of the Christian themes found within the data. I will finish with recommendations for youth

---

2. Ibid., 3. Italics in original.

ministry practitioners and implications this work might have for the field of youth ministry.

Because Young Life, from their origins, began ministry seeking young people where they were, establishing their ministry on what worked with high school students, I found it important to begin research by looking at the human experience of the organization from the perspective of experience. Because Young Life communicates their Christian message through stories, practical theology becomes the structure utilized to articulate their doctrinal stance. As Elaine Graham argued, Christian organizations generate theology through community.[3] I based my project on the idea that Young Life, as a Christian community, has produced a specific theology distinct for their organization. In chapter one, I outlined the qualitative methodology that I adapted in order to gather the data that would indicate the Christian understanding of Young Life in a rich and substantial way. Yin's theory of triangulation[4] allowed me to gather data from a diverse spectrum, ranging from historical documents, interviews, observation, as well as stories and symbols as found in the *Young Life* magazine. It was important to gather information from multiple points in order to form a rich tapestry of stories in order to produce a multidimensional understanding of the Young Life belief and expression of Christianity. Cultural studies[5] provided the backdrop for reading the "text between the lines" of both the words and images of the *Young Life* magazine, which was the main source of data, allowing for an articulation of their proclamation of God.

Emerging youth ministries in the 1940s were utilizing teenage youth culture to shape their outreach. Because of the split between fundamental and mainline denominations, independent evangelical youth ministries like Youth for Christ, InterVarsity Christian Fellowship, and Young Life were formed in parallel manner. These ministries utilized emerging trends such as the evolving understanding of adolescence, the teenage consumer culture, as well as post-WWII revivals to shape and structure their ministry to young people. However, I argued Young Life was innovative in practice as they sought to reach young people both in the world in which they inhabited (the local high school, sports fields, and hang out locations), as well as by speaking the language of faith in a manner they

3. Graham, *Transforming Practice*.
4. Yin, *Case Study for Research*.
5. McRobbie, *Feminism and Youth Culture*; Storey, *Cultural Studies*; Ward, *God at the Mall*.

would understand. Through the influence of Lewis Sperry Chafer, founder Jim Rayburn shaped a ministry that would capture the attention of young people not through rules and regulations but through humor, adventure, and a Christianity based on joy. Thus the culture of Young Life was shaped. In this research I also provided a brushstroke of the expanse of the ministry today as Young Life seeks to reach young people through club and camp, places where humor and adventure are lived out. I outlined the resources that are needed to complete that task as well as the current emphasis of president Denny Rydberg. Rydberg's emphasis on statistics and growth of the ministry has shifted the focus from relational ministry to one based on numbers. Beginning in 1996, Rydberg's goal was to grow the Young Life organization four hundred percent, and he shaped the organization through training programs and focused messages according to those goals. Young Life, under Rydberg, continues to seek numerical growth through a new goal titled "Reaching the World of Kids." Though Young Life continues to seek after young people in the teenage culture of today, they have tightened their understanding of the proclamation of Christ rather than loosened it.

In chapter two I introduced the doctrinal statements that structure the Young Life organization. The Statement of Faith and the Non-Negotiable Gospel Proclamation document provide shape for the ministry. However, I proposed that there are other doctrinal proclamations that have formed the message of the ministry from the outset. For example, Young Life has formalized statements of faith that, however, were articulated at a much later time than their youth ministry peers. I argued that, along with theologian Ray Anderson, it was the praxis of the ministry that actually shaped the beliefs of Young Life.[6] By using archival material, I was able to articulate the Young Life understanding of basic Christian tenets. I provided evidence of the incarnational theology that forms the backdrop of all Young Life work. Young Life leaders, operating as "Jesus with skin on," move into the world of kids in order to present them with the message of Christ. This message forms the Christological understanding of the ministry—proclaiming Jesus Christ as the most important person and the central focus of all Young Life work. For Young Life, sin and salvation are understood in relational terms. Life is hopeless apart from a relationship with God and salvation becomes "life that really clicks" when you make a decision to live in community with Christ. I presented data that shows the thrust of the Young Life discipleship model through Campaigners. Here young people are again encouraged to

---

6. Anderson, *The Shape of Practical Theology*.

Conclusions and Recommendations

be in relationship—in this case with peers as they work out the issues of faith. However, Young Life has found it difficult to transition young people into communities of faith because of their tenuous relationship with the church. As I stated, Young Life has often been encouraged by the support of the church while at the same time frustrated by the misunderstanding of Young Life practices on the part of congregations. Young Life has long been a prophetic voice on behalf of youth ministry in light of what they deem a lack of understanding on behalf of mainstream churches in reaching young people for Christ. Rayburn considered the Young Life organization pioneers on the frontier of youth ministry and often found himself, and his organization, at odds with the established church. The mentality remains of Young Life leaders feeling frustrated that churches "just don't get it" in terms of relational youth ministry. However, in our post-modern world with the numeric decline in our mainstream denominations, perhaps it is time for both Young Life and the Church to make a more concerted effort of working together to serve young people well in introducing them to Jesus Christ and finding fertile soil for them to plant roots in the Christian faith. Finally, in chapter three, I presented the drawbacks of a loose foundational theology for the organization. Because of the lack of strong theological statements that gave shape to the practices of the ministry, theological disagreements have recently arisen within the organization. Through this theological discussion and disagreement I reemphasized that it is practical belonging rather than theological belonging that drives the Young Life ministry.

Young Life should be commended for their consistent articulation of incarnational ministry as the cornerstone of their outreach as it is embodied in the practical belonging Ray Anderson noted gave shape to their ministry. As Young Life has sought out and welcomed young people from all walks of life, I believe they have embodied the welcoming spirit of God. But, as articulated by Anderson, Young Life's understanding of ministry was established on the praxis of ministry rather than a theological understanding informing and giving shape to their practice.[7] Jim Rayburn and early Young Life leaders went to great lengths to establish relationships with young people, often driving hours in order to lead clubs in new communities across the state of Texas. But I believe this was done simultaneously with the heart of Christ for young people as well as for the concern of logistics. Rayburn attempted countless models of ministry until he discovered one that worked. Has the emphasis of Denny Rydberg's mission of growth

7. Ibid.

for Young Life forced them to seek young people wherever they can find them in order to make that numeric growth? There is often a tension in the organization between the passion for Christ and a praxis that works. I believe it is within the tone of the Young Life Non-Negotiable document that the uncomfortable relationship between theology and practice is revealed within their ministry.

My critique of the Young Life organization begins with the Non-Negotiable document—specifically within the tone of their proclamations. I believe Young Life would have been better served if they had simply changed the language of the document and framed the argument in a more positive language. From the outset this document *feels* like Young Life is drawing a line in the sand and establishing absolute boundaries that Young Life staff must adhere to. Young Life states the document is not to squelch creativity but to provide a foundation upon which to build. However, they state the Non-Negotiables are not suggestions but something all Young Life staff must agree to. I believe that if Young Life had changed the language of the document to read something like "The Foundations for Young Life's Gospel Proclamation" it would have made a difference in tone—one that might be more palatable. Instead the organization gives the impression of sounding like absolute authoritarians who are trying to maintain control of something that might be *out* of their control. Young Life has long excelled at what they deem "meeting kids where they are" and going to young people in the world they inhabit. They have had to maintain a creative and flexible ministry in order to do that. They have sought out young people at skate parks, roller skating rinks, malls, school campuses, etc. They also meet young people in their search for Christ, answering questions from the simple to the complex, vowing to walk with teenagers through their exploration of the Christian faith. However, with the authoritarian tone of the Non-Negotiable document, Young Life executives seem to take the flexible and creative nature out of the ministry—the very thing that has made Young Life unique and successful over the years. If Young Life would change the Non-Negotiable document to a foundational document, Young Life leaders would be able to position themselves on the theological foundations of the ministry and then proceed from there with the creative energy needed to engage young people with the message of Christ and conversations about faith.

My second area of critique takes up the position of proclaiming the person of Jesus in *every* message within Young Life (proclamation one in the Non-Negotiable document). Young Life establishes this position in the articles of the Statement of Faith that centers on a Trinitarian understanding of God. However, in my observations and understanding of Young Life, a Trinitarian explanation of the Christian faith rarely happens, and I fear that Young Life is in fact portraying a Jesus-centric faith. It is commendable that Young Life has taken up the mantle of Jim Rayburn when he encourages Young Life to stick to presenting Jesus and not to "major in the minors." However, I wonder if the simplicity of proclaiming Christ has only watered down the faith to a palatable state and has not given young people a deep and rich faith that will sustain them over a lifetime. Has the message of the Christian faith Young Life shares become so attractive—one that is "liked" by adults and young people—that it has lost the call to sacrificial living? What does it mean for young people, as new believers, to pick up their cross and follow Christ? As Christian Smith[8] and Kenda Creasy Dean[9] have shown, young people in the United States today are at risk of a faith that is, at best, Moralistic Therapeutic Deism. Is the simplistic message of Young Life contributing to the shallow faith exhibited in young adults today?

My third area of critique takes up points of the Non-Negotiable document that discuss the articulation of Christ's death on the cross as well as the statement that calls young people to confess Christ as Lord (proclamations three and five within the Non-Negotiable document). It is here that I find discontinuities within the Young Life organization. On one hand they recognize the sinful brokenness of humanity that Christ suffered on our behalf on the cross. They emphasize the importance of proclaiming this clearly for young people to understand. Young Life, in practice, makes room for those who are physically and cognitively challenged (perhaps a vision of our suffering humanity) through their Capernaum ministry. However, there is a possibility that those who participate in Capernaum ministry might not be able to make the confession of faith in Christ that Young Life establishes as a firm point in their document of proclamation. What message does Young Life send to those suffering in all walks of life when they proclaim an attractive Christianity? Is this an example of their practical belonging but not their theological belonging? Are they giving two different messages to two different groups of people?

The argument for attractive Christianity is expressed in chapter four. I laid out this cultural Christian message of the organization as found in

8. Smith, *Soul Searching*.
9. Dean, *Almost Christian*.

archival material, specifically the *Young Life* magazine. Here I expressed Young Life presents an attractive Christianity through their use of images, humor, and casual language. They present a Christianity that "isn't for sissies," and they portray a faith that will make you better and stronger if you believe. I also presented evidence of the patriotic faith that weaves its way through Young Life publications. Through stories of the military and government, Young Life articulates a message of being an American Christian. And from the beginning of the ministry, all of these could be experienced at Young Life camp where you will "have the best week of your life." It is important to remember that, despite the change in decade, the material presents consistent themes carried throughout the Young Life organization no matter what the time. This chapter presents the message of Christianity as presented by Young Life in convergent ways—with photographs of couples in canoes combined with the strong message of the attractiveness of Christianity that pervaded the written content in the ministry in the early decades of their existence. Were marital difficulties for founder Jim Rayburn a factor in portraying faith in this light? Does Young Life present a romantic faith that attracts young people at the stage in their life where hormones are exploding? Does an "attractive" Christ deny the suffering servant that Jesus is? This chapter also highlights the strength of the Christian lifestyle by focusing on articles of athletics. The article titled "God Scored Our Touchdowns," and interviews with football player Don Moumaw illustrate the triumphal emphasis Young Life places on Christianity.

In chapter four I also presented the themes of Christianity as found in archival material as it is embodied on the local level of Holland Area Young Life club. Here I gave an overview of the structure of the Young Life ministry. Organizing the ministry around 5 C's, Young Life seeks to reach young people through contact work, club, camp, Campaigners, and the committee work of adults. I presented anecdotal evidence of Jack—a volunteer Young Life leader who embodies the incarnational and relational stance of the ministry. Through his work with a group of high school boys, Jack seeks to present the person of Christ in a way that makes most sense to them. Through the interview with Jack and subsequent information from the Holland Area Director, I was able to show the perspective on the Church and church partners that form a portion of the Young Life ministry. I also gave evidence of the themes of humor, fun, and casual language as it appeared in Holland High School club. Through the club talk given by Stacy, I showed evidence of the casual language in the proclamation of Christ that gives shape to the Young Life ministry. Jesus is referred to as "dude" and is one that can carry your burdens and fulfill the potential of your life. It is all through grace, which Stacy presented as one of the most important words of Christianity, though she did not present the term until the end of her talk.

I have presented evidence of the role casual language has played in the attractive Christianity Young Life presents. Through the decades of Young Life ministry the message of Christianity has been couched in the language of the times. The Prodigal Son story uses phrases for police like "the fuzz," "fella," and "old man," volunteer leaders understand casual language to be that which will attract young people to listen to the message of Jesus, but what does watering down the person of Jesus into "dude" do to his authority and divinity? Rayburn argued that Jesus was the most attractive, manly and loveable person he knew, but is Jesus diminished to yet another good-looking man that appeared on the cover of the *Young Life* magazine? Former Young Life staff person Anne Cheairs and interim president Ted Johnson both emphasized the importance of proclamation within Young Life, but does an informal and friendly proclamation actually conceal basic Christian doctrine that Young Life is actually trying to communicate?

However, in the midst of my challenges to the organization, I commend to Young Life their approach to Christian camping that places the high school young person at the center of its focus. Young Life strives to provide an environment that will be comfortable for a young person to hear a presentation of the gospel in a clear manner. They seek to capture the imagination of young people who may be anesthetized to gimmicks and schemes in today's culture. They seek to treat young people in a respectful manner, and in my opinion, I don't believe that happens on a regular basis in society today. However, I again challenge the organization to think more broadly about treating young people with the utmost of respect. If young people are the centerpiece of the ministry and Young Life is striving to proclaim a Christianity that will capture their imaginations, a deeper, more richly sophisticated theology will strengthen the faith of the young person carrying them into the future of their faith.

As I stated in the introduction, one of the driving forces of this research project was to discover the theological foundations from which the Young Life ministry operates. Incarnational theology has long been a guiding scaffold that has given structure for the Young Life organization. They have striven to be in the world of teenagers in order to present the message of Jesus to them through word and action. However, through the process of research and a serendipitous theological argument, I discovered I was not the only one who intuitively felt Young Life could be strengthened with a deeper or more comfortably held theological position that moved beyond incarnational theology. Ray Anderson perfectly articulated what I understand—Young Life has thrived in practical belonging but struggles with theological belonging. But practical belonging is one aspect of the Young Life organization that is a unique contribution to the field of evangelical youth ministry. The Young Life incarnational and relational approach to ministry honors the position of young people. The Young Life methodology of "going where kids are" reveals the heart of the organization—they desire to be in the world of young people in order to present the person of Christ in a manner that they will understand. However, there are risks to an incarnational ministry where adult leaders are considered "Jesus with skin on." Founder Jim Rayburn is an example of the difficult and tenuous combination of a human follower of Christ as he sought to share the good news of the gospel with high school students while struggling with addiction and marital strife. If the incarnational theology that informs the Young Life ministry is not married to other Christian theological tenets, I fear Young Life leaders will themselves believe *they* are ones that need to be attractive, humorous, strong, and relational instead of Christ bearing those burdens. Yes, Young Life embodies a very important and powerful message to the human need of young people—they have a place to belong in Young Life. But belonging must be the beginning of their journey with Christ and not the end. It is not enough that there are more and more numbers of teenagers participating in the ministry, fulfilling goals set out by the president of the organization. Young Life must strive for enriching and challenging young people with Christian growth and understanding.

The Young Life organization retains the fingerprint of founder Jim Rayburn in the manner in which they operate the ministry to this day. Rayburn fashioned an evangelical youth ministry that was innovative, practically, in relational ministry, striving to articulate an attractive Christianity. Young Life continues to strive to make Christ and Christianity attractive to young people through entertaining club, adventurous camp, and meaningful relationships through contact work. Club continues to utilize casual language that young people understand to present the person of Christ. Jim Rayburn was known for the way in which he spoke to young people in a manner that was current with teenagers of his day. Young Life has the opportunity to continue to reach thousands of unbelieving young people

Conclusions and Recommendations

if they would be willing to remain open to the new horizons of thinking in our post-modern world. It will be important for Young Life to maintain the essence of what has made the organization what it is today while adapting to the questions and conversations young people are seeking and the creative efforts Young Life leaders are taking to answer them. I wonder if those in authority in Young Life are uncomfortable with those trying to push the boundaries within the organization because Young Life, as a whole, was supposed to be the rebel against the organized church. Now, perhaps, Young Life has become so settled in who they are that they are unable to adapt as an organization to the trends and needs of adolescents in a post-modern world. Young Life, at the outset of their ministry, consistently challenged the Church to do youth ministry better.

And now I challenge Young Life with a similar sentiment—let's do youth ministry better. Therefore I recommend that Young Life embrace a theological position that welcomes and affirms a theological breadth and depth that allows leaders to present Jesus Christ in creative and innovative ways. Young Life has prided themselves on "reaching kids where they're at" and in this postmodern world that may mean a deeper theological world. I recommend that, as Young Life has perfected a practical belonging, they make strides in embracing a theological understanding of their youth ministry.

The implications of this work go beyond the bounds of the Young Life organization to the realm of youth ministry and practical theology as a whole. This project is a means of using practical theology as an analytical construct to look at the institutional history of one organization, Young Life, but could be adapted to investigate the theological articulation of any organization. I set out to discover how Young Life articulated their beliefs about God, and that through various ways of written and embodied forms. I have applied Graham's theory of practical theology as a means of understanding communal theological discourse. I have extended the discussion of practical theology to study an organization in a broad sense—looking at the history, current practice, and organizational discussion to provide an articulation of belief. My study provides at least one framework for utilizing practical theology, in all its multifaceted ways, for organizational analysis.

But the implications of this study do not only impact practical theology on a broad scale but on youth ministry as well. Youth ministry, an entity in and of itself, is worthy of specific research, understanding, and articulation. Using Young Life as an example, youth ministry has long been understood as an arena that is more interested in *what* works with young people rather than *why* youth ministers engage in the activities that they do. It is my hope that this project will give the field of youth ministry the permission to not only engage in praxis that reaches the world of teenagers with the Good News of Christ but will also understand and articulate the theological reasoning for doing so. Practical theology and youth ministry must be approached in a dialogical manner. Here I echo the sentiments of Douglas John Hall and Edward Farley—that the realities of faith are not established simply by theology but also with participation in communities of faith.[10] Hall states, "[T]he community of faith will wither and die—or suffer still more questionable fates—unless it is continuously nurtured by *theologia*." And this theology is not one narrowly designated for the field of theological training, but a theology that is one of *habitus*, one that belongs to the whole community of faith.[11] Youth ministry, as a field, must retain this understanding of theology and practice if it is to retain purposeful vision and action in this new millennium. This study has put into practice the theory of Graham who believed faith communities themselves could be generators of theology.[12] I have attempted to articulate what that looks like when applied to a specific ministry, and I have done that in order to strengthen an understanding of Young Life but also youth ministry in general. What has been done well in youth ministry in the past? What do we need to strengthen in the future so our young people have a faith that will allow them to thrive?

Douglas John Hall articulates what my journey has been through the process of this research project. He states, "On the other hand, the faith can be *thought*—that is, such reflection can become in the strict sense *theology*—only if, in the process of remembering all that precedes and excludes 'us,' we are simultaneously brought into a more articulate awareness of ourselves, our own identity, our 'situations in life' . . . ."[13] In thinking deeply about the Young Life organization, their history, the ways in which they articulate their beliefs about God, I have come to a better understanding of my personal theological beliefs. My understanding of youth ministry has been forged and shaped by my experience with Young Life—I have a relational understanding of youth ministry, one that values meeting young people where they are in their lives, pushing and stretching them through

10. Farley, various.
11. Hall, *Thinking the Faith*, 257.
12. Graham, *Transforming Practice*.
13. Hall, *Thinking the Faith*, 14.

experiences, and walking with them as they learn and grow with God. But I have also grown beyond my original boundaries of Young Life—I desire to root young people in a rich and historic faith that is a beautiful tapestry of stories of God's faithfulness to humanity, a faith that is broad and deep and will be a strong anchor point for young people to hold on to and be built into as their lives are joined to God's. This project has become a theological one for me as I have become more articulate in the ways in which Young Life has shaped me, but also the trajectory my work now takes with young people because of my intention to theologically anchor my ministry with them. I will conclude where I began with the words of Raymond Williams: "Wherever we have started from, we need to listen to others who started from a different position. We need to consider every attachment, every value, with our whole attention; for we do not know the future, we can never be certain of what may enrich it; we can only, now, listen to and consider whatever may be offered and take up what we can."[14]

The Way Forward

As I stated in the introduction, I began this search looking for answers to the practical difference in approach to youth ministry with adolescents inside and outside of the church. Having been shaped by the ministry and work of Young Life both in high school and college I set out to articulate the formal and informal theological foundations of the organization that I have deep respect for. My search led me towards historical documents, observations from the field, and theological disagreements from the public arena.

I continue to hold high esteem for a ministry that strives to present Jesus Christ to adolescents who have not heard the Good News of God's relationship with humanity in the midst of our rebellion. However, it is my belief that Young Life, and perhaps youth ministries within and outside of the Church, are doing a disservice to young people if they are not capable of reaching people on the farthest edges—even theological ones. Over the course of their history Young Life has continued to proclaim that they are doing the work that the Church has not stepped up to do, namely reaching adolescents who have no connection or desire to be a part of the Church or to follow the person of Jesus Christ. They hold the mindset that they will "meet kids where they're at" but refuse to step beyond a controlled and limited theological position in order to reach young people in a creative and

14. Williams, *Cultural Studies Reader*, 172.

strategic manner in the twenty-first century. It is my belief that Young Life could be doing prophetic and energizing work if leaders were allowed to adapt their message of Christ for the communities in which they work and articulate a message that their young people would understand. In the early years of parachurch youth ministry in the United States Young Life was one of the pioneers of creative and dynamic outreach to teenagers across the country. But with the recent theological disagreement that has hindered the cohesion of the ministry it is my fear that they are retreating into safe pasture of what has been done before rather than maintaining their spirit of bold work with teenagers leading them to the edges of society where the Good News could truly make headway in the lives of young people.

But rather than point fingers I believe Young Life can continue to enliven and influence ministry with youth around the world. They desire to serve young people well and in a manner that honors and celebrates the personhood of adolescence. Too often work within youth ministries in a congregational setting limits and isolates the young person from the community. That is not the Young Life way. They gather loving and supporting adults around their work, seek to engage the young person in their lives, and strives to raise up peer-leaders—all with a dynamic and energizing faith that is not ashamed of the gospel. Rather than lose sight of young people in the meld of birth-to-death discipleship, how would engaged and purposeful ministry with young people within the Church impact it today? I do not know the future of the Young Life ministry, but it is my hope that the themes considered here might in some way enrich the ministry for the future. It is my hope that as I have explored the culture of Young Life things might be taken up and will contribute in a lasting way. May it be so.

Bibliography

Agar, Michael H. *Speaking of Ethnography*. London: Sage, 1986.
Ammerman, Nancy. *Bible Believers: Fundamentalists in the Modern World*. New Brunswick, NJ: Rutgers University Press, 1987.
———. *Congregation and Community*. New Brunswick, NJ: Rutgers University Press, 1997.
———. "Just What Is Postmodernity and What Difference Does It Make to People of Faith?" The 1998 Princeton Lectures on Youth, Culture, and Church. Princeton Theological Seminary, 11–20.
Anderson, Ray. S. *The Shape of Practical Theology*. Downers Grove, IL: InterVarsity, 2001.
Bass, Dorothy. *Practicing Our Faith: A Way of Life for a Searching People*. San Francisco: Jossey-Bass, 1997.
Bass, Dorothy, and Volf, Miroslav. *Practicing Theology: Beliefs and Practices in Christian Life*. Grand Rapids: Eerdmans, 2002.
Berkhof, Hendrikus. *Christian Faith: An Introduction to the Study of Faith*. Grand Rapids: Eerdmans, 1986.
Borg, Marcus J. *Meeting Jesus Again for the First Time: The Historical Jesus and the Heart of Contemporary Faith*. San Francisco: HarperCollins, 1994.
Borgman, Dean. *When Kumbaya Is Not Enough: A Practical Theology for Youth Ministry*. Peabody, MA: Hendrickson, 1997.
Borgman, Dean, and Christine Cook, eds. *Agenda for Youth Ministry: Cultural Themes in Faith and Church*. London: Triangle, SPCK, 1998.
Browning, Don. *A Fundamental Practical Theology*. Minneapolis: Fortress, 1991.
———. *Practical Theology*. San Francisco: Harper & Row, 1983.
Cailliet, Emilie. *Young Life*. New York: Harper & Row, 1963.
Carpenter, Joel. *Revive Us Again: The Reawakening of American Fundamentalism*. New York: Oxford University Press, 1999.
Carroll, Jackson, et al, eds. *Handbook for Congregational Studies*. Nashville: Abingdon, 1986.
Chafer, Lewis Sperry. *He That Is Spiritual: A Classic Study of the Biblical Doctrine of Spirituality*. Grand Rapids: Zondervan, 1978.
Cicourel, Aaron V. *The Social Organization of Juvenile Justice*. Portsmouth, NH: Heinemann Educational, 1968.

Bibliography

Collins, Kenneth J. *The Evangelical Movement: The Promise of an American Religion.* Grand Rapids: Baker Academic, 2005.

Cook, Robert, and Torrey Maynard Johnson. *Reaching Youth for Christ.* Chicago: Moody Bible Institute, 1945.

Dart, John. "Young Life Draws Fire Over New Ministry Guidelines." *Christian Century*, January 15, 2008. http://www.christiancentury.org/article/2008-01/young-life-draws-fire-over-new-ministry-guidelines.

Dawn, Marva J. "Education as Commodity or Formation?" *Reformed Review* 57 (2003) 25–38.

Dean, Kenda Creasy. *Almost Christian: What the Faith of Our Teenagers Is Telling the American Church.* New York: Oxford University Press, 2010.

———. *The Godbearing Life: The Art of Soul Tending for Youth Ministry.* Nashville: Upper Room, 1998.

———. *Practicing Passion: Youth and the Quest for a Passionate Church.* Grand Rapids: Eerdmans, 2004.

———. "Proclaiming Salvation: Youth Ministry for the Twenty-first Century Church." *Theology Today* 56 (2000) 524–29.

Dean, Kenda Creasy, et al., eds. *Starting Right: Thinking Theologically about Youth Ministry.* Grand Rapids: Zondervan, 2001.

Denzin, Norma K. and Yvonne S. Lincoln, eds. *Collecting and Interpreting Qualitative Materials.* Thousand Oaks, CA: Sage, 2003.

Dorsey, Garey. *Congregation: The Journey Back to Church.* Cleveland: Pilgrim, 1995.

Dunlop, Sarah. *Visualising Hope: Exploring the Spirituality of Young People in Central and Eastern Europe.* Cambridge: YTC, 2008.

Dykstra, Craig. *Growing in the Life of Faith: Education and Christian Practices.* Louisville: Geneva, 1999.

Farley, Edward. *Ecclesial Man: A Social Phenomenology of Faith and Reality.* Philadelphia: Fortress, 1975.

———. *Practicing Gospel: Unconventional Thoughts on the Church's Ministry.* Louisville: John Knox, 2003.

———. *Theologia: The Fragmentation and Unity of Theological Education.* Philadelphia: Fortress, 1983.

Geertz, Clifford. *The Interpretation of Cultures.* New York: Basic Books, 1973.

Goffman, Erving. *Forms of Talk.* Oxford: Basil Blackwell, 1981.

Graham, Elaine. *Transforming Practice: Pastoral Theology in an Age of Uncertainty.* London: Mowbray, 1996.

Guder, Darrell. *Be My Witnesses.* Grand Rapids: Eerdmans, 1985.

Gustafson, James. *Treasure in Earthen Vessels.* Chicago: University of Chicago Press, 1961.

Hall, Douglas John. *Thinking the Faith: Christian Theology in a North American Context.* Minneapolis: Fortress, 1991.

Hansen, Collin. "Gospel Talk." *Christianity Today*, January 7, 2008, 13.

Hart, D. G., ed. *Reckoning With the Past: Historical Essays on American Evangelicalism from the Institute for the Study of American Evangelicals.* Grand Rapids: Baker, 1995.

———. *That Old-Time Religion in Modern America: Evangelical Protestantism in the Twentieth Century.* Lanham, MD: Ivan R. Dee, 2002.

Hartley, Jean. "Case Study Research." In *Essential Guide to Qualitative Methods in Organizational Research*, edited by Catherine Cassell and Gillian Symon, 323–33. London: Sage, 2004.

Bibliography

Hatch, Nathan O. *The Democratization of American Christianity*. New Haven: Yale University Press, 1989.

Heitink, G. *Practical Theology: History, Theory, Action Domains*. Studies in Practical Theology. Grand Rapids: Eerdmans, 1993.

Hickford, Andy. "What Is a Theology of Youth Ministry?" *Christian Education Journal* 16 (1996) 39–51.

Hine, Thomas. *The Rise and Fall of the American Teenager*. New York: Perennial, 1999.

Hopewell, James. *Congregation: Stories and Structures*. Philadelphia: Fortress, 1987.

Howe, Neil, and William Strauss. *Millenials Rising: The Next Great Generation*. New York: Vintage, 2000.

Hunt, Keith, and Gladys Hunt. *For Christ and the University: The Story of InterVarsity Christian Fellowship*. Downers Grove, IL: InterVarsity, 1991.

Hunter, James Davison. *American Evangelicalism: Conservative Religion and the Quandary of Modernity*. New Brunswick, NJ: Rutgers University Press, 1983.

Immink, F. Gerrit. *Faith: A Practical Theological Reconstruction*. Grand Rapids: Eerdmans, 2005.

Johnson, B. "The Spirituality of Education." *Reformed Review* 57 (2003) 39–52.

Jones, Tony. *Tony J*. 2008. http://www.tonyj.net.

Jones, W. Paul. *Worlds Within a Congregation: Dealing With Theological Diversity*. Nashville: Abingdon, 2000.

Jorgensen, Danny L. *Participant Observation: A Methodology for Human Studies*. Applied Social Research Methods 15. Newbury Park, CA: Sage, 1989.

Kett, Joseph. *Rites of Passage: Adolescence in America 1790 to the Present*. New York: Basic Books, 1977.

Kosanovich, W. T. "Confirmation and American Presbyterians." *Affirmation* 2 (1989) 40–64.

Kujawa, Sheryl, ed. *Disorganized Religion: The Evangelization of Youth and Young Adults*. Boston: Cowley, 1998.

Lanker, Jason. "Starting Right: Thinking Theologically about Youth Ministry." *Christian Education Journal* 4 (2007) 194.

Larson, Mel. *Youth for Christ: Twentieth Century Wonder*. Grand Rapids: Zondervan, 1947.

Lawler, M. G., and G. S. Risch. *Practical Theology: Perspectives from the Plains*. Omaha, NE: Creighton University Press, 2000.

Lee, Philip. J. *Against the Protestant Gnostics*. New York: Oxford University Press, 1987.

Lytch, Carol E. *Choosing Church: What Makes a Difference for Teens*. Louisville: Geneva, 2004.

Marsden, George, ed. *Evangelicalism and Modern America*. Grand Rapids: Eerdmans, 1984.

———. *Fundamentalism and American Culture*. New York: Oxford University Press, 2006.

———. "Fundamentalism as an American Phenomenon." In *Reckoning With the Past: Historical Essays on American Evangelicalism from the Institute for the Study of American Evangelicals*, edited by D. G. Hart, 303–21. Grand Rapids: Baker, 1995.

———. *Reforming Fundamentalism: Fuller Seminary and the New Evangelicalism*. Grand Rapids: Eerdmans, 1995.

———. *Religion and American Culture*. 2nd ed. Andover, UK: Cengage Learning, 2000.

Bibliography

Martinson, Roland D. *Effective Youth Ministry: A Congregational Approach*. Minneapolis: Augsburg, 1988.

Marty, Martin. "'Who Is Jesus Christ for Us Today?' as Asked by Young People" and "Youth between Late Modernity and Postmodernity." The 1998 Princeton Lectures on Youth, Culture, and Church, Princeton Theological Seminary, 21–36.

Marty, Martin, and R. Scott Appleby, eds. *Accounting for Fundamentalisms: The Dynamic Character of Movements*. The Fundamentalism Project 4. Chicago: University of Chicago Press, 1993.

May, Lary, *Recasting America: Culture and Politics in the Age of Cold War*. Chicago: University of Chicago Press, 1988.

McLaren, Brian D. *A New Kind of Christian: A Tale of Two Friends on a Spiritual Journey*. San Francisco: Jossey-Bass, 2001.

McRobbie, Angie. *Feminism and Youth Culture*. New York: Macmillan, 1991.

McSwain, Jeff. "Jesus Is the Gospel." E-mail of paper to Gretchen Schoon Tanis, September 2007.

———. "Young Life and the Gospel of All-Along Belonging." *The Other Journal*, January 2010. http://theotherjournal.com/2010/01/06/young-life-and-the-gospel-of-all-along-belonging/.

Meredith, Char. *It's a Sin to Bore a Kid: The Story of Young Life*. Waco, TX: Word, 1978.

Milbank, John. *Theology and Social Theory*. Oxford: Blackwell, 1990.

Miller, John. *Back to the Basics of Young Life*. Colorado Springs, CO: Young Life, 1991.

Miller, Randolph, Lee, and James Michael, eds. *Theologies of Religious Education*. Birmingham, AL: Religious Education, 1995.

Mudge, Lewis S., and James N. Poling, eds. *Formation and Reflection: The Promise of Practical Theology*. Philadelphia: Fortress, 1987.

Myers, Ken. *All God's Children and Blue Suede Shoes: Christians and Popular Culture*. Wheaton, IL: Crossway, 1989.

Myers, William R. "Church in the World: Models of Youth Ministry." *Theology Today* 44 (1987) 103–10.

———. *Research in Ministry*. Chicago: Exploration, 1993.

Nel, Malan. "Why Theology? It Is Only Youth Ministry." *Journal of Youth and Theology* 4 (2005) 9–22.

Nessan, Craig L. "Confirmation as Youth Ministry: The Task of Christian Formation." *Currents in Theology and Mission* 22 (1995) 269–74.

Nishioka, Rodger. "Forgiveness." In *Way to Live: Christian Practices for Teens*, edited by Dorothy C. Bass and Don C. Richter. Nashville: Upper Room, 2001.

———. *The Roots of Who We Are*. Louisville: Bridge Resources, 1997.

———. *Sowing the Seeds*. Louisville: Bridge Resources, 1998.

Osmer, Richard Robert. "Challenges to Youth Ministry in the Mainline Churches: Thought Provokers." *Affirmation* 2 (1989) 1–25.

———. *Confirmation*. Louisville: Geneva, 1996.

Osmer, Richard Robert, and Friedrich Schweitzer. *Religious Education between Modernization and Globalization: New Perspectives on the United States and Germany*. Grand Rapids: Eerdmans, 2003.

Pahl, Jon. *Shopping Malls and Other Sacred Places: Putting God in Place*. Grand Rapids: Brazos, 2003.

———. *Youth Ministry in Modern America: 1930 to the Present*. Peabody, MA: Hendrickson, 2000.

Bibliography

Palladino, Grace. *Teenagers: An American History*. New York: Basic Books, 1996.

Peterson, Eugene H. "The Exodus Propaedeutic for Spiritual Formation." *Reformed Review* 57 (2003) 63–74.

Poling, James Newton. *The Abuse of Power*. Nashville: Abingdon, 1991.

———. *Foundations for a Practical Theology of Ministry*. Nashville: Abingdon, 1985.

Proffitt, Anabel. "The Congregation as Educator." *Religious Education* 92 (1997) 294–415.

Rahn, Dave. "What Kind of Education Do Youth Ministers Need?" *Christian Education Journal* 16 (1996) 81–89.

Rayburn, Jim. Chicago Fellowship transcript. 1962.

———. *Monday Morning* letter. November 17, 1952.

Rayburn, Jim, III. *Dance, Children, Dance*. Wheaton, IL: Tyndale House, 1984, 2000.

Rice, Wayne, et al. *New Directions for Youth Ministry*. Loveland, CO: Group Publishing, 1998.

Richards, Lawrence O. *A Theology of Christian Education*. Grand Rapids: Zondervan, 1979.

Richter, Don C., et al. "Reconceiving Youth Ministry." *Religious Education* 93 (1998) 340–57.

Roebben, Bert. "Shaping a Playground for Transcendence: Postmodern Youth Ministry as a Radical Challenge." *Religious Education* 92 (1997) 332–47.

Root, Andrew. *Revisiting Relational Youth Ministry*. Downers Grove, IL: InterVarsity, 2007.

Schleiermacher, Friedrich. *A Brief Outline of the Study of Theology*. Translated by Terrence N. Tice. Richmond: John Knox, 1966.

———. *Christian Caring*. Translated by James O. Duke and Howard Stone. Philadelphia: Fortress, 1988.

Schultze, Quentin, and Roy Anker, eds. *Dancing in the Dark: Youth, Popular Culture and the Electronic Media*. Grand Rapids: Eerdmans, 1991.

Senter, Mark, III. *The Coming Revolution in Youth Ministry*. Wheaton, IL: Victor, 1992.

Senter, Mark, III, et al., eds. *Four Views of Youth Ministry and the Church*. Grand Rapids: Zondervan, 2001.

Shaw, Ian Graham Ronald. *Qualitative Evaluation*. Introducing Qualitative Methods. London: Sage, 1999.

Shelley, Bruce. "The Rise of Evangelical Youth Movements." *Fides et Historia* 18 (1986) 47–63.

Shelley, Marshall. *Helping Those Who Don't Want Help*. Waco, TX: Words, 1986.

Silverman, David. *Doing Qualitative Research: A Practical Handbook*. 2nd ed. London: Sage, 2005.

Smith, Christian. *American Evangelicalism: Embattled and Thriving*. Chicago: University of Chicago Press, 1998.

———. *Soul Searching: The Religious and Spiritual Lives of American Teenagers*. New York: Oxford University Press, 2005.

Smith, Christian, and D. Campbell. "Why the New Young Life 'Non-Negotiable' Statement on Gospel Proclamation Needs to Be Re-considered." E-mail of paper to Gretchen Schoon Tanis, 2007.

Spradley, James P. *The Ethnographic Interview*. Belmont, CA: Wadsworth, 1979.

Starr, Bill. Letters to executive board of Young Life, 1966, 1968, 1973, 1977.

Stone, Howard, and James Duke. *How to Think Theologically*. Minneapolis: Augsburg, 2006.

Bibliography

Storey, John, ed. *Cultural Theory and Popular Culture.* 2nd ed. Athens: University of Georgia Press, 2003.
Sublett, Kit, ed. *The Diaries of Jim Rayburn.* Houston: Whitecaps Media, 2008.
Sweet, Leonard. *Postmodern Pilgrims.* Nashville: Broadman and Holman, 2000.
———. *Quantum Spirituality: A Postmodern Apologetic.* Dayton, OH: Whaleprints, 1991.
Swinton, John, and Harriet Mowat. *Practical Theology and Qualitative Research.* London: SCM, 2006.
Tanner, Kathryn. *Theories of Culture: A New Agenda for Theology.* Minneapolis: Fortress, 1997.
Turnage, Lynn. *Growing a Group.* Louisville: Bridge Resources, 1998.
Tuttle, Bob. *Growing Leaders. Roots of Youth Ministry.* Louisville: Bridge Resources, 1998.
Van Maanen, John. *Tales of the Field: On Writing Ethnography.* Chicago: University of Chicago Press, 1988.
Volf, Miroslav, and Dorothy C. Bass, eds. *Practicing Theology.* Grand Rapids: Eerdmans, 2002.
Ward, Pete. *God at the Mall.* Peabody, MA: Hendrickson, 1999.
———. *Liquid Church.* Peabody, MA: Hendrickson, 2002.
———. *Relational Youthwork.* Oxford: Lynx Communications, 1997.
Webber, Robert. *Ancient-Future Faith: Rethinking Evangelicalism for a Postmodern World.* Grand Rapids: Baker, 1999.
Williams, Raymond. *Cultural Studies Reader: History, Theory, Practice.* New York: Longmans, 1995.
Willimon, William. "Imitating Christ in a Postmodern World: Young Disciples Today." The 1998 Princeton Lectures on Youth, Culture, and Church, Princeton Theological Seminary, 79–89.
Wind, James P., and James W. Lewis. *American Congregations: New Perspectives in the Study of Congregations.* Chicago: University of Chicago Press, 1994.
Wolf, Richard G. "Implementing a Community-based Model for Youth Ministry." *Chicago Theological Seminary Register* 84 (1994) 1–13.
Woodward, James, and Steven Pattison, eds. *The Blackwell Reader in Pastoral and Practical Theology.* Oxford: Blackwell, 2000.
Woolever, Cynthia, and Deborah Bruce. *Beyond the Ordinary: Ten Strengths of U.S. Congregations.* Louisville: Westminster John Knox, 2004.
Wright, Dana, and J. Keuntzel. *Redemptive Transformation in Practical Theology: Essays in Honor of James E. Loder Jr.* Grand Rapids: Eerdmans, 2004.
Wuthnow, Robert. *Crises in the Churches.* New York: Oxford University Press, 1997.
———. *The Struggle for America's Soul.* Grand Rapids: Eerdmans, 1989.
Wyckoff, D. Campbell, ed. *Religious Education Ministry with Youth.* Birmingham, AL: Religious Education, 1985.
Yaconelli, Mark. "Focusing Youth Ministry through Christian Practice." In *Starting Right: Thinking Theologically about Youth Ministry,* edited by Kenda Creasy Dean et al., 155–65. Grand Rapids: Zondervan, 2001.
———. "Youth Ministry: A Contemplative Approach." *Christian Century* 116, April 1999, 450–54.
Yates, Rick. *Skits for Camp and Club.* http://www.younglife.org. 2010.
Yin, Robert K. *Case Study Research: Design and Methods.* 2nd ed. Applied Social Research Methods 5. Thousand Oaks, CA: Sage, 1994.
Young Life. Business card and logo. 2008.

Bibliography

Young Life. *Focus on Youth* magazine. 1967: October; 1968: January; 1969: January; 1972: Summer, Fall; 1974: Summer; 1975: Spring, Winter; 1976: Fall.

Young Life. Informational Booklet. 1965.

Young Life. Leadership Training Manual. 1994.

Young Life. "Non-Negotiables of Young Life's Gospel Proclamation." http://www.younglife.org. 2007.

Young Life. *Relationships* magazine. 1987: June/July, August, December; 1989: June; 1990: Spring; 1992: Spring; 1993: Spring, Fall; 1994: Summer; 1995: Fall; 1997: January/February; 1998: Fall/Winter; 1999: Spring/Summer; 2000: Spring, Summer; 2002: Spring, Summer; 2003: Winter; 2004: Fall, Winter; 2005: Fall, Winter; 2006: Fall, Winter; 2007: Spring; 2009: Spring, Winter; 2010: Spring.

Young Life. *Road Trip: A Journey Along the Road to Real with Your Friends,* 2007.

Young Life. "Statement of Faith." http://www.younglife.org.

Young Life. Training Manual. 1969.

Young Life. *Young Life.* http://www.younglife.org/us. 2010.

Young Life. *Young Life* magazine. 1944: February, March, May, September, October, December; 1945: January, February, March, June, September; 1946: February, March, June, July, August, October; 1947: July, February, March, May, July, June; 1948: February, March, April, May, June, July; 1949: June; 1950: June, October; 1951: January, February, March, June, July, October, November; 1952: April, May, June, September, November, December; 1953: January, March, April, September, October, November, December; 1954: March, June, July; 1955: January, March, May; 1956: January, May, July, August, October; 1957: January, February, December; 1958: March, July, September; 1959: April, October; 1960: February, May, August.

Young Life. Year-End Report, 1970–1971, 1971–1972, 1974.

Young Life Foundation: *Reaching Out* magazine, 1987.

www.ingramcontent.com/pod-product-compliance
Lightning Source LLC
Chambersburg PA
CBHW071458150426
43191CB00008B/1387